Mark Krueger
Editor

MW01274661

Themes and Stories
in Youthwork Practice

Themes and Stories in Youthwork Practice has been co-published simultaneously as *Child & Youth Services*, Volume 26, Number 1 2004.

Pre-publication
REVIEWS,
COMMENTARIES,
EVALUATIONS . . .

"RICH. . . .VALUABLE. . . . HIGHLY RECOMMENDED FOR EVERY LEVEL OF YOUTH-WORKER. . . .Describes the experience of youthwork from the perspective of a capable worker. This is a major accomplishment because it is so readable and transparent for less skilled workers, who may be new to the field or haven't had the benefit of competent supervisors and co-workers. THIS IS A TEXT FOR NEW STUDENTS AND A DISCUSSION SEMINAR FOR MATURE PRAC-TITIONERS AT THE SAME TIME."

Jack Phelan, MS
Certified CYC Worker
Program Co-Chair
CYC Program
Grant MacEwan College
Alberta, Canada

"IF YOU EVER WANTED TO KNOW WHAT YOUTH CARE WORK IS, YOU SHOULD READ THIS BOOK. If you ever wondered what it *can* be, you should read it again. USEFUL TO THE PRACTITIONER, STUDENT, OR TEACHER interested in discovering the depth of this work, this book offers a refreshing perspective from the traditional control and authority approaches so common in our field. It presents youthwork as a living, vibrant, and personal experience of discovery for the youth and the worker. If you don't read it you are missing something important in your own education and development. It defines the possibilities of the field. In an eloquent and lyrical fashion, Krueger and his associates lead us through the experience that is youthwork. This book is not for the superficial. It is for those who are truly interested in exploring the depth of this experience that we call youthwork."

Thom Garfat, PhD
Co-editor of CYC-Net International *and Relational* Child and Youth Care Practice
Editor of A Child and Youth Care Approach to Working with Families

"COMPELLING AND ENGAGING. . . .Those who feel that we have lost the way in thinking about and working with youth, as control, procedures, rejection, and rigidity seem to have taken precedence over caring, flexibility, and meaningful relationships, will be warmed and inspired by this book. A particularly strong feature of this book is that it is clear in its intent and offers a specific conceptual framework with examples."

Karen VanderVen, PhD
*Professor of Psychology in Education
University of Pittsburgh*

The Haworth Press, Inc.

Themes and Stories
in Youthwork Practice

Themes and Stories in Youthwork Practice has been co-published simultaneously as *Child & Youth Services*, Volume 26, Number 1 2004.

The *Child & Youth Services*™ Monographic "Separates"

Below is a list of "separates," which in serials librarianship means a special issue simultaneously published as a special journal issue or double-issue *and* as a "separate" hardbound monograph. (This is a format which we also call a "DocuSerial.")

"Separates" are published because specialized libraries or professionals may wish to purchase a specific thematic issue by itself in a format which can be separately cataloged and shelved, as opposed to purchasing the journal on an on-going basis. Faculty members may also more easily consider a "separate" for classroom adoption.

"Separates" are carefully classified separately with the major book jobbers so that the journal tie-in can be noted on new book order slips to avoid duplicate purchasing.

You may wish to visit Haworth's website at . . .

http://www.HaworthPress.com

. . . to search our online catalog for complete tables of contents of these separates and related publications.

You may also call 1-800-HAWORTH (outside US/Canada: 607-722-5857), or Fax 1-800-895-0582 (outside US/Canada: 607-771-0012), or e-mail at:

docdelivery@haworthpress.com

Themes and Stories in Youthwork Practice, edited by Mark Krueger (Vol. 26, No. 1, 2004). *"If you ever wanted to know what youth care work is, you should read this book. If you ever wondered what it can be, you should read it again. Useful to the practitioner, student, or teacher interested in discovering the depth of this work, this book offers a refreshing perspective from the traditional control and authority approaches so common in our field. It presents youth work as a living, vibrant, and personal experience of discovery for the youth and the worker. If you don't read it you are missing something important in your own education and development. It defines the possibilities of the field. In an eloquent and lyrical fashion, Krueger and his associates lead us through the experience that is youth work. This book is not for the superficial. It is for those who are truly interested in exploring the depth of this experience that we call youth work."* (Thom Garfat, PhD, Co-editor of CYC-Net International *and* Relational Child and Youth Care Practice; Editor of A Child and Youth Care Approach to Working with Families)

A Child and Youth Care Approach to Working with Families, edited by Thom Garfat, PhD (Vol. 25, No. 1/2, 2003). *"From ethics to data, from activities to support groups, from frontline to being in family homes—it's all here."* (Karl W. Gompf, BSc, MA, Consultant in Child and Youth Care, Red River College, Winnipeg, Manitoba, Canada)

Pain, Normality, and the Struggle for Congruence: Reinterpreting Residental Care for Children and Youth, James P. Anglin (Vol. 24, No. 1/2, 2002). *"Residential care practitioners, planners, and researchers will find much of value in this richly detailed monograph. Dr. Anglin's work adds considerably to our understanding of the residential care milieu as a crucible for change, as well as a scaffolding of support that transects community, child, and family."* (James Whitaker, PhD, Professor of Social Work, The University of Washington, Seattle)

Residential Child Care Staff Selection: Choose with Care, Meredith Kiraly (Vol. 23, No. 1/2, 2001). *"Meredith Kiraly is to be congratulated. . . . A lucid, readable book that presents the fruits of international experience and research relevant to the assessment and selection of child care workers, and which does so in a way that leads to practical strategies for achieving improvements in this important field. This book should be read by anyone responsible for selection into child care roles."* (Clive Fletcher, PhD, FBPsS, Emeritus Professor of Occupational Psychology, Goldsmiths' College, University of London; Managing Director, Personnel Assessment Limited)

Innovative Approaches in Working with Children and Youth: New Lessons from the Kibbutz, edited by Yuval Dror (Vol. 22, No. 1/2, 2001). *"Excellent. . . . Offers rich descriptions of Israel's varied and sustained efforts to use the educational and social life of the kibbutz to supply emotional and intellectual support for youngsters with a variety of special needs. An excellent supplement to any education course that explores approaches to serving disadvantaged children at risk of failing both academically and in terms of becoming contributing members of society."* (Steve Jacobson, PhD, Professor, Department of Educational Leadership and Policy, University of Buffalo, New York)

Working with Children on the Streets of Brazil: Politics and Practice, Walter de Oliveira, PhD (Vol. 21, No. 1/2, 2000). Working with Children on the Streets of Brazil *is both a scholarly work on the phenomenon of homeless children and a rousing call to action that will remind you of the reasons you chose to work in social services.*

Intergenerational Programs: Understanding What We Have Created, Valerie S. Kuehne, PhD (Vol. 20, No. 1/2, 1999).

Caring on the Streets: A Study of Detached Youthworkers, Jacquelyn Kay Thompson (Vol. 19, No. 2, 1999).

Boarding Schools at the Crossroads of Change: The Influence of Residential Education Institutions on National and Societal Development, Yitzhak Kashti (Vol. 19, No. 1, 1998). *"This book is an essential, applicable historical reference for those interested in positively molding the social future of the world's troubled youth." (Juvenile and Family Court Journal)*

The Occupational Experience of Residential Child and Youth Care Workers: Caring and Its Discontents, edited by Mordecai Arieli, PhD (Vol. 18, No. 2, 1997). *"Introduces the social reality of residential child and youth care as viewed by care workers, examining the problem of tension between workers and residents and how workers cope with stress." (Book News, Inc.)*

The Anthropology of Child and Youth Care Work, edited by Rivka A. Eisikovits, PhD (Vol. 18, No. 1, 1996). *"A fascinating combination of rich ethnographies from the occupational field of residential child and youth care and the challenging social paradigm of cultural perspective." (Mordecai Arieli, PhD, Senior Teacher, Educational Policy and Organization Department, Tel-Aviv University, Israel)*

Travels in the Trench Between Child Welfare Theory and Practice: A Case Study of Failed Promises and Prospects for Renewal, George Thomas, PhD, MSW (Vol. 17, No. 1/2, 1994). *"Thomas musters enough research and common sense to blow any proponent out of the water.... Here is a person of real integrity, speaking the sort of truth that makes self-serving administrators and governments quail." (Australian New Zealand Journal of Family Therapy)*

Negotiating Positive Identity in a Group Care Community: Reclaiming Uprooted Youth, Zvi Levy (Vol. 16, No. 2, 1993). *"This book will interest theoreticians, practitioners, and policymakers in child and youth care, teachers, and rehabilitation counselors. Recommended for academic and health science center library collections." (Academic Library Book Review)*

Information Systems in Child, Youth, and Family Agencies: Planning, Implementation, and Service Enhancement, edited by Anthony J. Grasso, DSW, and Irwin Epstein, PhD (Vol. 16, No. 1, 1993). *"Valuable to anyone interested in the design and the implementation of a Management Information System (MIS) in a social service agency..." (John G. Orme, PhD, Associate Professor, College of Social Work, University of Tennessee)*

Assessing Child Maltreatment Reports: The Problem of False Allegations, edited by Michael Robin, MPH, ACSW (Vol. 15, No. 2, 1991). *"A thoughtful contribution to the public debate about how to fix the beleaguered system ... It should also be required reading in courses in child welfare." (Science Books & Films)*

People Care in Institutions: A Conceptual Schema and Its Application, edited by Yochanan Wozner, DSW (Vol. 14, No. 2, 1990). *"Provides ample information by which the effectiveness of internats and the life of staff and internees can be improved." (Residential Treatment for Children & Youth)*

Being in Child Care: A Journey Into Self, edited by Gerry Fewster, PhD (Vol. 14, No. 2, 1990). *"Evocative and provocative. Reading this absolutely compelling work provides a transformational experience in which one finds oneself alternately joyful, angry, puzzled, illuminated, warmed, chilled." (Karen VanderVen, PhD, Professor, Program in Child Development and Child Care, School of Social Work, University of Pittsburgh)*

Homeless Children: The Watchers and the Waiters, edited by Nancy Boxill, PhD (Vol. 14, No. 1, 1990). *"Fill[s] a gap in the popular and professional literature on homelessness.... Policymakers, program developers, and social welfare practitioners will find it particularly useful." (Science Books & Films)*

Perspectives in Professional Child and Youth Care, edited by James P. Anglin, MSW, Carey J. Denholm, PhD, Roy V. Ferguson, PhD, and Alan R. Pence, PhD (Vol. 13, No. 1/2, 1990). *"Reinforced by empirical research and clear conceptual thinking, as well as the recognition of the relevance of personal transformation in understanding quality care." (Virginia Child Protection Newsletter)*

Specialist Foster Family Care: A Normalizing Experience, edited by Burt Galaway, PhD, MS, and Joe Hudson, PhD, MSW (Vol. 12, No. 1/2, 1989). *"A useful and practical book for policymakers and professionals interested in learning about the benefits of treatment foster care." (Ira M. Schwartz, MSW, Professor and Director, Center for the Study of Youth Policy, The University of Michigan School of Social Work)*

Helping the Youthful Offender: Individual and Group Therapies That Work, edited by William B. Lewis, PhD (Vol. 11, No. 2, 1991). *"In a reader-friendly and often humorous style, Lewis explains the multilevel approach that he deems necessary for effective treatment of delinquents within an institutional context." (Criminal Justice Review)*

Family Perspectives in Child and Youth Services, edited by David H. Olson, PhD (Vol. 11, No. 1, 1989). *"An excellent diagnostic tool to use with families and an excellent training tool for our family therapy students. . . . It also offers an excellent model for parent training." (Peter Maynard, PhD, Department of Human Development, University of Rhode Island)*

Transitioning Exceptional Children and Youth into the Community: Research and Practice, edited by Ennio Cipani, PhD (Vol. 10, No. 2, 1989). *"Excellent set of chapters. A very fine contribution to the literature. Excellent text." (T. F. McLaughlin, PhD, Department of Special Education, Gonzaga University)*

Assaultive Youth: Responding to Physical Assaultiveness in Residential, Community, and Health Care Settings, edited by Joel Kupfersmid, PhD, and Roberta Monkman, PhD (Vol. 10, No. 1, 1988). *"At last here is a book written by professionals who do direct care with assaultive youth and can give practical advice." (Vicki L. Agee, PhD, Director of Correctional Services, New Life Youth Services, Lantana, Florida)*

Developmental Group Care of Children and Youth: Concepts and Practice, Henry W. Maier, PhD (Vol. 9, No. 2, 1988). *"An excellent guide for those who plan to devote their professional careers to the group care of children and adolescents." (Journal of Developmental and Behavioral Pediatrics)*

The Black Adolescent Parent, edited by Stanley F. Battle, PhD, MPH (Vol. 9, No. 1, 1987). *"A sound and insightful perspective on black adolescent sexuality and parenting." (Child Welfare)*

Qualitative Research and Evaluation in Group Care, edited by Rivka A. Eisikovits, PhD, and Yitzhak Kashti, PhD (Vol. 8, No. 3/4, 1987). *"Well worth reading. . . . should be read by any nurse involved in formally evaluating her care setting." (Nursing Times)*

Helping Delinquents Change: A Treatment Manual of Social Learning Approaches, Jerome S. Stumphauzer, PhD (Vol. 8, No. 1/2, 1986). *"The best I have seen in the juvenile and criminal justice field in the past 46 years. It is pragmatic and creative in its recommended treatment approaches, on target concerning the many aspects of juvenile handling that have failed, and quite honest in assessing and advocating which practices seem to be working reasonably well." (Corrections Today)*

Residential Group Care in Community Context: Insights from the Israeli Experience, edited by Zvi Eisikovits, PhD, and Jerome Beker, EdD (Vol. 7, No. 3/4, 1986). *A variety of highly effective group care settings in Israel are examined, with suggestions for improving care in the United States.*

Adolescents, Literature, and Work with Youth, edited by J. Pamela Weiner, MPH, and Ruth M. Stein, PhD (Vol. 7, No. 1/2, 1985). *"A variety of thought-provoking ways of looking at adolescent literature." (Harvard Educational Review)*

Young Girls: A Portrait of Adolescence Reprint Edition, Gisela Konopka, DSW (Vol. 6, No. 3/4, 1985). *"A sensitive affirmation of today's young women and a clear recognition of the complex adjustments they face in contemporary society." (School Counselor)*

Adolescent Substance Abuse: A Guide to Prevention and Treatment, edited by Richard E. Isralowitz and Mark Singer (Vol. 6, No. 1/2, 1983). *"A valuable tool for those working with adolescent substance misusers." (Journal of Studies on Alcohol)*

Monographs "Separates" list continued at the back

Themes and Stories in Youthwork Practice

Mark Krueger
Editor

Themes and Stories in Youthwork Practice has been co-published simultaneously as *Child & Youth Services*, Volume 26, Number 1 2004.

The Haworth Press, Inc.

New York • London • Victoria (AU)
www.HaworthPress.com

Themes and Stories in Youthwork Practice has been co-published simultaneously as *Child & Youth Services*™, Volume 26, Number 1 2004.

The development, preparation, and publication of this work has been undertaken with great care. However, the publisher, employees, editors, and agents of The Haworth Press and all imprints of The Haworth Press, Inc. including The Haworth Medical Press® and Pharmaceutical Products Press®, are not responsible for any errors contained herein or for consequences that may ensue from use of materials or information contained in this work. Opinions expressed by the author(s) are not necessarily those of The Haworth Press, Inc. With regard to case studies, identities and circumstances of individuals discussed herein have been changed to protect confidentiality. Any resemblance to actual persons, living or dead, is entirely coincidental.

The Haworth Press, Inc., 10 Alice Street, Binghamton, NY 13904-1580 USA

Cover design by Marylouise E. Doyle

Library of Congress Cataloging-in-Publication Data

Krueger, Mark.
    Themes and stories in youthwork practice / Mark Krueger.
        p. cm.
"Co-published simultaneously as Child & youth services, volume 26, number 1 2004."
Includes bibliographical references and index.
    ISBN 0-7890-2581-7 (hard cover : alk. paper) – ISBN 0-7890-2582-5 (soft cover : alk. paper)
1. Social work with youth. 2. Counselor and client. I. Child & youth services. II. Title.
HV1421.K785 2004
362.7'083–dc22
                                                                            2004019308

Indexing, Abstracting & Website/Internet Coverage

This section provides you with a list of major indexing & abstracting services. That is to say, each service began covering this periodical during the year noted in the right column. Most Websites which are listed below have indicated that they will either post, disseminate, compile, archive, cite or alert their own Website users with research-based content from this work. (This list is as current as the copyright date of this publication.)

Abstracting, Website/Indexing Coverage . . . . Year When Coverage Began

- *AIDS and Cancer Research <http://www.csa.com>* 1990
- *Biosciences Information Service of Biological Abstracts (BIOSIS)*
  a centralized source of life science information
  <http://www.biosis.org> 1983
- *Business Source Corporate: coverage of nearly 3,350 quality*
  magazines and journals; designed to meet the diverse
  information needs of corporations; EBSCO Publishing
  <http://www.epnet.com/corporate/bsourcecorp.asp> 2001
- *Child Development Abstracts & Bibliography*
  (in print & online) <http://www.ukans.edu> 1982
- *CINAHL (Cumulative Index to Nursing & Allied Health Literature)*
  in print, EBSCO, and SilverPlatter, Data-Star, and PaperChase.
  (Support materials include Subject Heading List, Database Search
  Guide, and instructional video) <http://www.cinahl.com>. 2001
- *Criminal Justice Abstracts* 1982
- *Educational Research Abstracts (ERA) (online database)*
  <http://www.tandf.co.uk/era>. 2002
- *e-psyche, LLC <http://www.e-psyche.net>* 2001
- *Exceptional Child Education Resources (ECER), (CD-ROM*
  from SilverPlatter and hard copy)
  <http://www.ericec.org/ecer-db.html> 1982

(continued)

(continued)

Special Bibliographic Notes related to special journal issues
(separates) and indexing/abstracting:

- indexing/abstracting services in this list will also cover material in any "separate" that is co-published simultaneously with Haworth's special thematic journal issue or DocuSerial. Indexing/abstracting usually covers material at the article/chapter level.
- monographic co-editions are intended for either non-subscribers or libraries which intend to purchase a second copy for their circulating collections.
- monographic co-editions are reported to all jobbers/wholesalers/approval plans. The source journal is listed as the "series" to assist the prevention of duplicate purchasing in the same manner utilized for books-in-series.
- to facilitate user/access services all indexing/abstracting services are encouraged to utilize the co-indexing entry note indicated at the bottom of the first page of each article/chapter/contribution.
- this is intended to assist a library user of any reference tool (whether print, electronic, online, or CD-ROM) to locate the monographic version if the library has purchased this version but not a subscription to the source journal.
- individual articles/chapters in any Haworth publication are also available through the Haworth Document Delivery Service (HDDS).

Themes and Stories
in Youthwork Practice

CONTENTS

ABOUT THE EDITOR

Mark Krueger, PhD, is Professor and Director of the Youth Work Learning Center at the University of Wisconsin in Milwaukee. He helped found the research and education center for youthworkers in 1979. Prior to that, he spent 11 years as a youthworker in two residential centers for troubled youths. Dr. Krueger has written nine books, including two novels and a book of short stories about youthwork, all of which are focused on improving youthwork practice. Some of the titles are *Intervention Techniques for Child and Youth Care Workers, Job Satisfaction for Child and Youth Care Workers, Careless to Caring for Troubled Youth, Floating* (novel), *In Motion* (novel), *Buckets: Sketches from a Youth Worker's Logbook*, and *Nexus: A Book About Youth Work.* Dr. Krueger has also made several contributions to research journals, and he has been an active participant in the movement to professionalize youthwork throughout his career including serving as president of state and national associations of child and youth care workers. He has received several international and national awards for his contributions to the field.

Preface

Stories have played a significant role in the development of the child and youth care field from the beginning, not only stories as activities that engage the interests and animate the imaginations of young people in group care but also stories that illuminate the development of the field, build its sense of shared identity, and inform its practice. Almost from the beginning, Mark Krueger has been our storyteller *par excellence,* one whose own practice and writings have been largely story-based. And now we have a volume that encapsulates his contributions, presenting some of his most captivating old and new stories of practice and building on them to develop and present the linkages between our stories and effective developmentally oriented child and youth care practice.

The stories in this volume, really mostly vignettes, which come from the experiences of the editor's colleagues as well as his own, capture the pace, the process, and the passion of child and youth care work. Krueger applies the metaphor of modern dance, as he has done before, to illuminate the performance of the effective worker, schooled in technique and able to adapt and apply it spontaneously, "on the fly," constantly improvising as the immediate situation requires. The work is not pre-scripted but rather represents an emerging choreography in which each step is determined by what preceded it.

In the basketball story early in the volume, Krueger neatly portrays the need for workers to operate on two levels at the same time. They must be "into" the game to be able to relate to the youth authentically and convincingly, yet at the same time always aware of their role as caring adults with developmental objectives for their work. This and other important practice principles are illuminated by the stories, and the reader needs to be alert to what he or she can learn from each one, just as child and youth care workers need to listen with a "third ear" (thanks to

[Haworth co-indexing entry note]: "Preface." Beker, Jerome. Co-published simultaneously in *Child & Youth Services* (The Haworth Press, Inc.) Vol. 26, No. 1, 2004, pp. xiii-xiv; and: *Themes and Stories in Youthwork Practice* (ed: Mark Krueger) The Haworth Press, Inc., 2004, pp. xiii-xiv. Single or multiple copies of this article are available for a fee from The Haworth Document Delivery Service [1-800-HAWORTH, 9:00 a.m. - 5:00 p.m. (EST). E-mail address: docdelivery@haworthpress.com].

xiii

Theodor Reik for the term) to understand what youth are saying to them behind the words and through their behavior.

But Krueger does not leave all the work to the reader. He provides 25 themes such as "Being Present," "Body Language," "Touch," "Silence," "Atmosphere and Place," "Transitions," and "Just Being," all illustrated through stories. He also provides examples of interpretation and analysis of stories by child and youth care workers, followed by a reservoir of additional stories with personal sketches by the writers that tell us something about who they are. The final chapter presents three longer stories by the editor, which he views as "works in progress," that begin to integrate his personal and professional development as a child and youth care worker. Amidst the stories, the editor also introduces discussion of how they have been and can be used, including by practitioners, to advance research about group care and the professional preparation of child and youth care workers. The volume concludes with a long and useful reference list.

So this is a storybook in the best sense of the term. It presents real stories by child and youth care workers in a wide range of settings, reflecting their everyday work lives, the routine events and the crises that are the "stuff" of the job, and how they respond. It draws on the stories to illustrate the nuances of effective practice, and it describes and demonstrates how story-based education and research can contribute to the growing sophistication and professionalization of the field. All of us who read it can emerge as wiser, more sensitive child and youth care workers, and better storytellers as well!

Enjoy!

Jerome Beker
University of Minnesota

Acknowledgments

Special thanks are due to the youthworkers and their stories. Thanks also to Gerry Fewster, Leon Fulcher, Thom Garfat, Henry Maier, and Karen Vander Ven, who reviewed the book while it was in progress. Their comments and suggestions were instrumental in the organization, substance, and shape of the material. Their writing also inspired much of the thinking that went into the book.

Some of the stories in the book appeared in our monthly column in the *CYC-Net.org* online magazine and the *Journal of Child and Youth Care*. We appreciate the editors' willingness to allow us to share the stories again.

Introduction

This volume presents a way of thinking about and studying youthwork. It suggests that youthworkers, like modern dancers, plan (choreograph) their shifts in advance, bring themselves and their skills to the moment, and improvise along the way. It also supports the notion that one way to understand youthwork is through story–our own stories, youth stories, and the stories youthworkers and youth construct together as they dance.

The volume has four parts: Chapter one, "Youthwork as Modern Dance," narrates one day in youthwork and a description of youthwork as modern dance. A qualitative inquiry, "Using Self and Story to Understand Youthwork," including youthworkers' stories, is presented in the second chapter. More of the youthworkers' stories follow in the third chapter, "Moments with Youth." The last chapter, "Three Sketches," shows how I have been exploring my experiences.

Mark Krueger

NOTE

The term youthworker is used as a generic term for child and youth care workers, youth development workers, and others who work with youth in community centers, group homes, treatment centers and a number of other community and group care programs. Youthwork is what youthworkers do and the focus of this volume.

[Haworth co-indexing entry note]: "Introduction." Krueger, Mark. Co-published simultaneously in *Child & Youth Services* (The Haworth Press, Inc.) Vol. 26, No. 1, 2004, p. 1; and: *Themes and Stories in Youthwork Practice* (ed: Mark Krueger) The Haworth Press, Inc., 2004, p. 1. Single or multiple copies of this article are available for a fee from The Haworth Document Delivery Service [1-800-HAWORTH, 9:00 a.m. - 5:00 p.m. (EST). E-mail address: docdelivery@haworthpress.com].

http://www.haworthpress.com/web/CYS
Digital Object Identifier: 10.1300/J024v26n01_01

Chapter One
Youthwork as Modern Dance

Nicole and Matt are working together at Nexus, the group home, with six youth: Cathie, Maria, Ramon, Ron, Cheryl, and Nick. Nexus is a two-story house in the center of a medium-sized city. It is an older building that has been decorated and enlivened with the youth's art and music.

Nicole is sitting with Cathie, Maria, and Ramon at the dining room table. She is teaching them how to manage money, a skill they will need when they leave the group home and live on their own.

"My parents never had a budget," Maria says.

"Neither did mine. They never sat down like this and wrote down how they would spend their money," Ramon says.

"Each family does it a little differently. My parents didn't do it quite like this, but I find it helpful myself to have a budget; otherwise I tend to spend more than I have," says Nicole.

"How can you spend more than you have?" Cathie asks.

"Charge cards."

"Yeah, I can't wait to get a charge card," Ramon says.

"Charge cards can be helpful, especially if you don't want to carry a lot of money; but they can also be a problem."

"How?" Maria asks.

"You spend more than you can pay back and get further and further in debt."

"We're leaving now," says Matt, as he walks through the dining room with Nick, Cheryl, and Ron. They are on their way to the play-

[Haworth co-indexing entry note]: "Youthwork as Modern Dance." Krueger, Mark. Co-published simultaneously in *Child & Youth Services* (The Haworth Press, Inc.) Vol. 26, No. 1, 2004, pp. 3-24; and: *Themes and Stories in Youthwork Practice* (ed: Mark Krueger) The Haworth Press, Inc., 2004, pp. 3-24. Single or multiple copies of this article are available for a fee from The Haworth Document Delivery Service [1-800-HAWORTH, 9:00 a.m. - 5:00 p.m. (EST). E-mail address: docdelivery@haworthpress.com].

ground to play basketball. It's a familiar walk, one they take together two or three times a week.

Nick is sad and worried. He's leaving the group home. In a few days he'll be going into independent living. Like the other youth in the program, at age 18 he will have to make in it on his own.

It's a warm fall day. They choose sides. Cheryl and Ron will play Nick and Matt. As they warm up with jumpers and hook shots, they playfully try to block each other's shots.

The early moments of the game go smoothly, as if choreographed by their history of playing together. They know and anticipate each other's moves. The score bounces back and forth. A shot is blocked, a rebound grabbed, a ball falls cleanly through the net.

During the game, similar to the way he works with them in other activities, Matt tries to get a sense of where each youth is and position himself in a way that he can help advance the game. After about 45 minutes of play, the score is tied. They take a break and drink from the jar of ice water Matt brought from the group home. Nick sits next to Matt on the asphalt with his back to the chain-link fence. As Cheryl and Ron stand nearby, ribbing one another about an errant pass or blocked shot, Nick begins to think again about his departure from the group home. Then he stands and knocks the ball out of Ron's hands, and the game is on again.

The pace intensifies. Matt and Nick stretch the lead, then the others catch up and go ahead. Nick shoves Ron as he goes for a loose ball. Ron turns and gets in Nick's face. "Cool it," Matt says, holding the ball. He waits until they back away from each other and throws the ball back into play.

Cheryl scores, putting her team ahead by four. Matt throws the inbounds pass to Nick in the corner. He goes up for a jumper. Ron times his leap perfectly and blocks the ball an instant after it leaves Nick's hand.

"Foul!" Nick shouts.

"Bull, it was clean," Ron responds, mocking Nick by imitating how he blocked the shot.

"Fuck you!"

Fists clenched by his side, Ron walks slowly toward Nick, and Matt steps in between them.

"He's just worried about leaving," Ron says.

"No I'm not, motha'-fucker," Nick responds.

Ron raises his fists and lunges forward, pretending he's ready to fight.

"Cool it, Ron! You too, Nick. Let's take a break," Matt says.

"I don't need to settle down. He fouled me." Nick points at Ron.

"Ron and Cheryl, take a few shots at the other end while I talk to Nick," Matt says as he motions for Nick to follow him to the side of the court.

"Why do I have to talk to you? He's the one who started it," says Nick.

Matt takes a drink of ice water and hands it to Nick. "Look, I understand about your leaving. I'm going to miss you, and so are the rest of the guys, but getting into it with Ron won't help. If you want to talk, I'm here to listen."

"I don't want to talk about it here."

"Okay, later then, but cool it for the rest of the game."

Nick looks down at his shoes.

"Nick," Matt says, waiting for a response.

Nick nods, reluctantly.

"Okay, let's get rolling," Matt shouts and the game regains its earlier rhythm. They play for about 15 more minutes. Cheryl and Ron win by a basket.

"Good game," Matt says, then looks at Nick and playfully bumps him on the shoulder.

"Yeah, good game," Nick says.

As they walk back, their pace slower now than before the game, Matt thinks about the difficulties of leaving for the residents: for those who leave and those who stay. Nick's leaving has probably stirred up similar feelings in Ron and Cheryl, who will leave in a few months. He shifts position to be closer to one youth, then another, and chats about dinner and the jazz television program they will watch after they do their homework.

The smell of tacos has filled the group home, a duplex that was converted a few years ago into a group home for youth transitioning to independent living. It is full of symbols of youth–posters, pictures, music and magazines–that say this is a place where young people live and this is who they are.

Cathie, Maria, and Ramon are in the kitchen with Nicole making dinner. This is one of many activities they engage in to develop the skills and feelings they will need when they live on their own. Throughout the day they do chores and develop skills that will help them when they get a full-time job. They also learn how to problem solve, open banking accounts, drive a car and talk about their feelings.

Maria and Nicole are chopping lettuce, tomatoes, onions, and green peppers for the tacos. Ramon is grating cheese. Cathie is frying ground beef.

"When will we eat? I'm starving," says Ron.

"In a few minutes. You can set the table," responds Nicole.

Nick, Matt, and Cheryl help Ron set the table while Nicole and the others put the food into bowls and set it on the table. Before they sit down, Matt lowers the volume of the music. Each meal begins by having one youth share something that happened during their day. Tonight it is Cheryl's turn. "Ron and I crushed Nick and Matt in two-on-two," she says, imitating a jumper by flicking her wrist in front of her face.

"Crushed us? What game were you playing in?" Matt jokes.

"Two ff-lousy points," says Nick, catching himself before he says the curse word.

"Pass the cheese, I'm starving," Ron says, preparing his taco. The bowls begin to move around the table, passed from one hand to another as the youth and workers build tacos. As the conversation and the meal take on a rhythm of their own, there is a sense of harmony, but then suddenly the rhythm is interrupted. "Give me that!" Ramon shouts at Maria.

Nicole looks at Ramon.

"She's hogging the tomatoes."

"Maria, pass Ramon the tomatoes," says Nicole.

The meal regains its flow. After dessert, they work together to clean up. There is some jostling, swearing, and playful teasing as they wash and dry the dishes together. Matt and Nicole treat each situation in context, ignoring some incidents and intervening in others. Then the youth go to their rooms to study.

During study hour, Matt and Nicole make sure that each youth gets individual attention as they question and praise the youth looking for moments of connection and discovery. "How do you think that problem might be solved?" Matt asks Maria, putting his hand on her shoulder as he stands behind Maria, who is at the desk in her room.

"What's another way of thinking about what that story means?" Nicole asks Ron as she sits with him in the living room reading a short story for his literature class.

After study hour they break into two groups. Cathie, Maria, and Ron go with Matt to watch a documentary on jazz, and the other three go with Nicole to the recreation room in the basement to continue work on a mural. The mural covers and circles the walls in the recreation room. Each youth is asked to add something that is an expression of him- or herself. What they paint is entirely up to them as long as they do it with respect for the work of the others and the spirit of the mural: no gang symbols, swearing, or scenes of graphic sex or violence. They work together but each in his or her own space.

"I like that, especially the color scheme," Nicole says to Cheryl.

"It's a mandala; we were learning about them in class," Cheryl says and explains what they are.

Upstairs the others are watching the documentary portraying the history of jazz and blues and its many leaders.

"I told you the brothers started rock and roll. Jazz, blues, then rock and roll. Elvis, this guy Benny Goodman–they were just along for the ride," Ron says.

"Yeah, but they got all the money," Cathie says.

"I never knew all this," Maria says.

"Man, where you been?" Ron replies.

Matt comes in with a bowl of popcorn, napkins, and soft drinks for each person. He's learning as much about music as the boys are.

"Hip hop comes from jazz," Ron says. "It all does."

Nicole pokes her head in the room. "I thought I smelled popcorn. I'll get the others and we'll join you."

"Good," says Matt.

Ron and Nick quickly fill their napkins with popcorn.

"I can make more; don't worry, there'll be plenty," Matt says.

The youth and workers sit together on the floor in harmony, eating popcorn and watching the rest of the show. Then it is time for bed. Nicole turns off the TV and picks up the empty bowl of popcorn. Matt turns on some quiet music. "Okay, let's go."

There is some playful pushing and shoving as the boys climb the stairs and take turns using the bathroom. Matt and Nicole help them straighten their things and get their materials ready for school.

"Lights out," Nicole says. Each youth slowly gets into bed. Ron and Ramon, roommates, like a little quiet music as they fall to sleep. Cheryl likes her room totally dark. Cathie and Maria leave the blinds open so the streetlight can shine through. Nick, like most youth when they are getting near the time to leave, has his own room.

Nicole and Matt spend a little time with each youth, giving them the attention they need. Some youth like to talk a little while others just need a friendly goodnight and, perhaps, a hand on the shoulder or cover pulled up to their chin. Nicole stops in Nick's room last. He's still reading.

"C'mon, time for lights out," Nicole says.

"I know, I was just reading a little longer. This book is hard to read, but it's really good," Nick says, referring to *A Portrait of the Artist as a Young Man.*

"Yes, it was hard for me too," says Nicole.

"The author is really trying to be himself, isn't he?"

"Yes. How are you doing?" She sets the book on the desk for Nick and turns off the reading light.

"Okay, I guess."

"Yeah, it's difficult, I know, but I think you're going to find your way too, and we'll be here if you need to come back to talk." Nicole catches herself: She tells herself to listen and not try to make things seem better–a weakness of hers.

"I know, but I'm still worried." Nick says.

Nicole pulls up a chair and listens as Nick talks about home and being on his own.

In another room, Matt talks to Cheryl, who has been sexually abused. "Will I ever find a man who will want and respect me?" she asks. Matt tries to assure her that she will.

YOUTHWORK AS MODERN DANCE

Imagine that Matt and Nicole are like modern dancers. Their shift is planned (choreographed) in advance but improvised along the way. As they interact, they try to sense as well as know when to be at the center of the group and at the edge, when to move in or move out, to raise or lower their voices, to walk or run, sit down or stand, and so forth.

Meanwhile, the youth learn to dance by being with Nicole and Matt. They begin to get a feel for where they should be, what they should do, and how they should speak in certain situations. Boundaries and limits are tested as they move closer or apart. Skills are learned such as brushing teeth, shooting a basket, painting a mural, or solving math problems as they move together through the day. A conflict is resolved as they struggle and find a sense of resolution.

As they dance, several themes define their attitudes, actions, and movements. These themes are interconnected. One overlaps with or is intertwined with another, a nexus or spaghetti bowl of values, beliefs, and approaches.

Choreographing the Dance

> We need to work with and relate to youth as unique developing be-
> ings. (Maier, 1987, pp. 2-4)

In preparing for their shift (choreographing), Nicole and Matt plan their interactions to be geared to the youth's developmental needs and strengths. For example, they consider factors such as the following: Nick, who is worried about his home visit, will need extra attention. Maria, Cathie, and Ramon will need help with budgeting. For Maria, who can make her bed, today might be a good day to do it with her. Ramon has a doctor's appointment so be alert that he might do something to avoid it. Although they are all getting better, mealtimes are still stressful, because most of them are not used to meals as a positive social experience (meals prior to coming to the group home were eaten alone, often in difficult circumstances, with lots of arguing). Tonight is tacos, which most of them like. Tomorrow will be something new that reflects the cultural background of another youth.

Basketball and mural painting will give them each a chance to participate in something that is compatible with their interests and skills. Ron can have a little extra space. He seems to be in good shape. Cathie, who was sexually abused, will still do anything to avoid being alone with her thoughts at bedtime and, as usual, will need to know that someone is available to talk to. And Nick, of course, will also need someone.

Being with Youth

> Youthworkers don't build trust, mechanically, like carpenters build houses . . . They are in the world with youth in a way that discloses trust as fundamental to being together as human beings. (Baizerman, 1992, pp. 129-133)

As they dance (interact) Matt and Nicole try to be *with* youth *in* the activities of daily living. They do their self-awareness homework in advance, then immerse themselves in a walk or chore or meal or dinner, offering self, hope, and possibility as they learn and grow together.

Being Present

> A continual theme I have learned from a valued co-worker and others is that to "show up" with youth (to be available and open to where the youth is at without a rigid agenda of what to discuss or do) is sometimes the most valuable thing one can do. (Amy Evans)

Matt and Nicole's presence is conveyed with eyes that are alert and attentive, a sense of enthusiasm about the task at hand, and the underlying message, "I am here and will go with you."

They should train their own mind to respond to what is happening on the inside and the outside in the moment while placing the client (youth) at the center of attention. (Fewster, 1999, p. 51)

Most of the time, Matt and Nicole are in the moment, focused on the youth, energetic, available, and self-aware but not self-consumed. Sometimes, however, they get distracted. Their minds are elsewhere. They are preoccupied with what to do next or with something that happened in the past or elsewhere. They catch themselves, re-focus, and struggle to maintain a delicate balance between being in the moment and thinking one step ahead.

Light on Their Feet

When I'm out of my head and lost in the movement of the dance, it opens me to letting in outside influences. And this is usually story . . . When I am doing something it is easier to lose myself and empathize with other people. (Willem Defoe, on the TV program, *Inside the Actor's Studio*)

Like Defoe, Matt and Nicole don't literally lose themselves but, rather, they try to be free to be engaged with youth and the task at hand. In these moments, when activity and self are one, they have "biking consciousness" or "talking consciousness" or "cooking consciousness" (Van Manen, 1990, p. 38).

For example, during the basketball game, the game seems to have a life of its own. Matt and the youth are lost in their movements. As Nicole and the youth paint the mural, time seems to pass unnoticed.

Moving with and in Time

As a result, one problematic element of making time primary is that the programmatic focus becomes "behavior," especially behavior that interferes with the schedule and our expectations for the use of time. (Magnuson, Baizerman, & Stringer, 2001, p. 304)

Time moves with them rather than forces them forward. A day or activity or period might begin and end at a certain time, but time does not drive them nor does outcome. They are not goal-focused but moving together towards a goal in a way that will get them there. In these moments, their motion, as Aristotle said, is the mode in which the future and present are one. They rake leaves, do dishes, or play basketball at a pace that will get them to the end of their chore or activity in good time.

Certain events, of course, are done on and within fixed time. Meals are at 5:00; basketball or art are from 3:00 to 4:00. Nicole and Matt teach the youth to respect time and to be timely as they search for a balance and try to keep time from governing their movements and actions. Youth learn to be on time, but even more importantly they learn to be present, their actions and movements embodying time itself (Magnuson, Baizerman, & Stringer, 2001).

Sometimes time is lost track of or they become fixed on time at the expense of allowing the needs of the youth and the activity to take the time it needs. They stop, say "Wait," and give it time.

Listening, Hearing and Seeing

The youth have Matt and Nicole's undivided attention. Matt listens at dinner, his eyes and ears focused on Ron, then Cheryl. "I'd really like to hear about it," he says.

It is too quiet. Nicole goes down the hall to see what's happening. Nick and Ron raise their voices in anger. Matt moves closer.

> The expressiveness of the individual (and therefore the capacity to give impressions) appears to have two radically different kinds of sign activity: the expressions that he gives and the impression that he gives off. (Goffman, 1959, p. 2)

Nick gets up from his chair and joins an activity. Matt walks beside him and says, "I'm glad you joined us."

Sometimes Matt and Nicole lose sight of what's happening. They do not hear what is really being said. The youth's actions remind them that something is missing: Look and listen.

Body Language

Matt and Nicole "walk the talk." Their bodies say, "I am excited, sad, angry, or happy." Their actions and feelings are consistent, and behavior and emotions convey a sense of awareness and genuineness.

Matt leans against the fence as he talks to one of the youth during the break from basketball, conveying a sense of relaxation, then later stands straight, feet planted as he tries to calm Nick in a firm, nonthreatening manner.

They should practice the art of mirroring–reflecting back their experience of the client (youth) free from any specific attention to affect or influence the experience of the client. (Fewster, 1999, p. 52)

"This is what I feel, hear, see. My affect, actions, and posture are reflections of what I feel inside and see in you," say Nicole's body, words, and actions during dinner and mural painting.

Curiosity

As they dance, Matt and Nicole's movements, actions, facial expressions, and attitudes say, "Tell me your story, I want to know you and how you are feeling."

"So, how did you feel when you gave your presentation in school today?" Matt asks Cheryl.

"What was it like at dinner at your house?" Nicole asks Ron.

Matt goes downstairs and looks at the mural. One by one he asks the youth to tell him about what they painted.

Proximity and Position

During the crafts program, I noted that Mike was starting to snap at Larry and that the latter was, in turn, beginning to look a little wild-eyed as he does before he has a squealing outburst coming on against someone . . . Accordingly, I shifted to the other side of the room so that I was considerably closer to the scene of action, prepared to intervene if necessary but not giving any other overt indication. (Redl & Wineman, 1952, p. 164)

Nicole, who sees, hears, and feels where she is in relationship to the members of the group, moves closer to Ramon and Cathie who seem to need her presence. Matt steps back. Ron needs some space. Nicole kneels down to talk with Cheryl, who is sitting on the floor, so their eyes can meet on the same level. Matt walks in the center of the group to the park, shifts position, and hangs back to talk with Nick.

Touch

I wish I could hug the kids more often, but I must be careful. I must learn small talk also, so I will not scare them. Some kids are afraid they might be melted away. They must be tough and put on a hard face. They have learned at a young age the hardening of the heart. (Phuc Nygen, 1992, p. 94)

With sensitivity to Ron's history and readiness for touch, Nicole hugs him good night, while Ramon gets a hand on the shoulder and Cheryl a simple, reassuring "Good night."

Matt and Nicole physically restrain one of the boys about to hurt another boy. They use a hold designed to secure but not hurt. Afterwards, they search for other ways to get close. They sit next to him on the couch or bump shoulders playfully on walks.

Matt feels and reads a youth's readiness to be touched. It takes courage. He understands that some youth, especially those who have been sexually abused, might interpret their touch as harmful. Thus he is cautious about how he touches but not afraid to touch when the time is right.

Silence

> By not saying anything I was letting him know that it was okay with me that he was angry and that I was not going to try to change him. (Molly Weingrod, this volume, ch. 2, p. 44)

Nicole and Matt pause, or stop themselves from responding, and let the youth search for the answer. They seek quiet time when they can share a moment or two of silence. Matt sits while quietly reading with a group of youth or takes a walk with a youth without saying anything.

Nicole senses a youth's fear or anxiety–and is anxious herself–but restrains herself from filling the void with words that will only heighten the anxiety, or she reminds herself that anxiety in this moment is okay and does not need to be fixed. "It's okay to be silent and experience this moment of anxiety," she tells herself.

The group is getting noisy. Matt asks for their attention and suggests a few moments of silence and breathing. He turns off the radio and sits down with them: "Let's just be here together a moment and enjoy the silence."

Speaking Across the Spaces of Their Experiences

> When you work with troubled children it is not their reality you wander, it is your own. (Garfat, 1991, p. 159)

"This is what it's like for me. What's it like for you?" Or, "Tell me how you see it," the workers say, speaking across the spaces of their experiences with youth (Garfat, 1998; Sarris, 1993). Maria shows that she is sad. Nicole changes her position, posture and facial expression, matching it to how she thinks Maria is feeling. A youth stands next to or sits with Nicole, or pulls away–depending on how he reads her response to his feelings. Nicole continues or tries something different.

> Those footprints you see around you are on the border of your own reality, not theirs. Tread gently and with caution but do not be led by your fear. For in the territory of the children's reality where it borders with your own, lies the opportunity for change, for them and you. (Garfat, 1991, p. 159)

All of the workers' resources are used–creativity, self-awareness, instincts, and intuition–as they feel their way through the day while searching for and finding new ways to understand themselves, the world around them, and each other.

Acting with Purpose

Each chore or activity or discussion has significance in the composition they create together during a shift. Making beds, talking, and doing dishes are the most meaningful things that can be done together in those moments.

"Tomorrow is Saturday. I'm really looking forward to cleaning the yard and the field trip," Matt says at dinner.

"I hate yard cleaning," Ron says.

Matt smiles. "It's just as important as the field trip. If we do it together, it can be fun. Besides, I think we'll feel even better about the field trip, knowing we got our work finished."

Immediacies

The day is full of immediacies–unpredictable and predictable events that need attention (Guttman, 1991). A fight breaks out. A homework assignment is lost 15 minutes before school. Four youth want attention at the same time. Chili is burning on the stove. A 15-year-old is sad, sitting by the window waiting for his parents, who are late for their visit.

Matt and Nicole respond to or ignore these events. Nicole moves between the youth who are fighting, decides to let a youth look for his own homework, turns off the stove, and sits silently next to the boy waiting for his visit, guided by her awareness of each youth's need or lack of need for her assistance. At times they are overwhelmed. They stop, take a deep breath and/or call for assistance, reminding themselves to set priorities.

Breathing

It was new–I found where I was going–arriving 1 hour early–I parked a few blocks away–turned off the car–practiced deep breathing and visualized myself in a sunny clearing by a waterfall. I approached the home–took deep breaths as I rang the door bell–the door opened–I saw his back as he walked away–"Watch out for the fucking dog"–I took a sip of coffee–moved forward–deep breathed–thinking to myself remember to breathe . . . (Joseph Stanley)

Matt pauses, takes a deep breath, centers himself, then moves again fueled by steady, even breathing.

They should begin with their own experience of their own body sense, using breathing to access and release the energies of the core Self. They should work to contain these energies within a boundary that can move toward contacting, without invading, another self. (Fewster, 1999, p. 51)

Rhythmic Interactions

Have you noticed that when people jog, dance, or throw a Frisbee in rhythm with one with each other, they seem to experience momentary bonding and a sense of unity? At these and other moments of joint rhythmic engagement, they discover an attraction for each other regardless of whether there has been a previous sense of caring. Rhythmic interactions forge people together. Rhythmicity provides a glue for human connections. (Maier, 1992, p. 7)

Matt and Nicole play, dance, and jog rhythmically with youth. Matt raises or lowers his voice, walks fast or slow, and sits down to set or reinforce the tempo for an activity or chore that is in synch with the youth's readiness and capacity to participate.

Sometimes they intentionally alter or change the rhythm to transition to a new activity or discontinue a present one. Nicole alters the cadence of her voice to get their attention as a situation begins to get out of hand, or she walks quickly to move the group from a period of inactivity or slows to begin to quiet the group as they walk to dinner.

When they are out of synch, they feel the tension or lack of response. Intuitively, Matt searches for a new beat or tempo, trying to regain a sense of togetherness.

> As everyone, adults and boys alike, takes a seat in the living room, a new calmer rhythm is set. The more harried pace of early morning activity is replaced by a slower, more relaxed tempo. Voice levels are softened, movements are not so hurried. It is the adults' responsibility to facilitate this change in the rhythms of the group. (Fahlberg, 1990, p. 172)

Atmosphere and Place

> Whatever space supports the endeavor, the question remains: in which way can spatial factors be altered to further accentuate the process? (Maier, 1987, p. 59)

Tone, mood, space, light, sound, and smell influence interactions. The dining room may be noisy or quiet and the play area too small–or the right size–for the number of participants. Matt raises or dims the lights, moves to a quieter place with a youth who is out of control, turns down the radio so they can talk while they are eating.

Nicole's mood helps set the tone. She is serious, sad, or excited based on what she feels, hears, and sees. Matt comes to work in a bad mood, but quickly tries to get out of it. With youth they try to create an atmosphere of excitement. They ask, "Is this a space where we can be together with enthusiasm and hope for the future and, if not, how can we change it?"

Walls are decorated with the youth's pictures of heroes and friends. Favorite colors and music are chosen. Decorations reflect the cultural diversity of the group. Maybe the atmosphere does not feel right. It is too cold or warm, too noisy or quiet, too isolated or crowded. Matt and Nicole make an adjustment.

> The wish to be periodically alone and to have a space of one's own is not merely a whim within children and adults; it is a human requirement. (Maier, 1987, pp. 59-62)

Private and public places are created and designated. Each place is respected. Murals, posters, paintings, colors, images, words, and sounds say, "This is our/my room. You can see, hear, and feel our/my presence in it." The living room and dining room in the group home are filled with expressions of the youth who currently reside there. Their pictures, drawings and colors are on display in places where they gather and share together. Each bedroom is different, an expression of the individuals who reside there.

Rules and attitudes say, "This is a place where you/we can be safe. We are committed to each other's well being."

Improvisation

Matt "plays off" the youth, letting his senses, instincts, and intuition guide him. Nicole is in the moment aware, breathing, hearing, seeing, sensing her proximity to the youth, and communicating with her body. She raises or lowers her voice, walks slow or fast, shifts position, sits and stands. She alters the composition each shift or moment, changes direction with a new activity or shift in tempo and mood. Sometimes their improvisations are slightly off. Despite their best efforts they are out of synch with the youth. They try again, searching for a shared tempo.

Transitions

Transitions tie events together and establish patterns of successful separation, change, and reconnection. The workers move with youth from chores to the art room, sleep to awake, school to after-school, and group home to home with a feel for the movement and an understanding of the meaning of preceding and following events. Time is left to end, begin, and move between. Events, if needed, are summed up and foreshadowed. A quick pace conveys enthusiasm, and a slow pace settles the group. The distance between the dancers is adjusted based on the need for closeness or distance.

Each transition is different and has a different meaning. A youth leaves the group home. Nicole offers a friendly, "See you when you get back," her voice reassuring as if to say, "Here, take part of this moment with you to make you safe."

A youth moves from passing a math test with excitement to swimming, from a supervised to a more independent level of activity, and from a good meal to continue a painting in the art room. Matt conveys a sense of enthusiasm while setting a pace and tone for successful movement and change.

Waiting and Anticipating

They wait, sit, pass time, anticipate, and share boredom. A parent is late for a visit, the line for the concert ticket is long, or the doctor is behind schedule. Matt helps a youth learn to accept waiting as something that cannot and should not be avoided as part of life. "We have to be patient now. Rushing will not make it happen sooner." Or "I know it is boring to just sit here, but this is part of life."

> Doing nothing is time in and on our hands. But doing nothing where something can happen is more interesting than being bored. There is nothing boring about anticipation. (Baizerman, 1995, p. 340)

Matt and Nicole engage youth in discussions about places they would like to be and/or hang. Then, when they are with youth in these places, they try to convey a sense of excitement about the future: "We are here, you and I, and it is exciting because we are in a place with a sense of possibility."

"Let's think about our activity tonight," Matt says as he waits with a youth on another occasion, sensing that the boredom is becoming too much.

Just Being

Sometimes they do something–or nothing–simply for the sake of doing or being. Their expectation is not outcome but rather to do or not do something that has a "life of its own." They are in an activity or moment with no intended outcome other than to just be there. They sit quietly, talk or walk together, or read alone just for the sake of doing it.

Recreational/Creative Expressive Activities

> "Each of our youth has a special activity interest and hobby," the agency director comments as she leads you into the day room of the group residential home. As you walk in you are stunned. You've never seen such an engaging scene. Several small groups of youth are seated around tables, each one with a worker nearby. One group is playing chess. Another group is working on a quilt, while another is carefully selecting and gluing tiles onto a mosaic grid. You overhear snatches of conversation, and sometimes even the occasional swear word seems appropriate for the activities at hand. "Shit man, that was some move you made." Looking up for a minute, your eye travels out the window and you see a flash of

color headed for the hoop of a basketball court. Then you hear a whistle: "Coaching instruction for our intramural team," explains the director. You then realize something smells good. "Kitchen detail," she says. "They're interested in cooking and are preparing tonight's snacks." (Vander Ven, 1999b, in "You Are What You Do and Become What You've Done," p. 133)

Matt and Nicole paint, sing, play ball, camp, dance, act, write poems, and tell stories with youth. Their canvases, productions, and compositions are part of the culture of daily living.

Nature is a prominent part of their activity. The outdoors is a stage for many of their performances. Trees, plants and water are props and sources of inspiration and learning. Together they learn and try to be with these things that are part of them. They get wet and dirty together as they swim and plant. The environment in which they interact enriches their lives. By being in and with nature they find fulfillment, inspiration, and unlimited sources of learning.

Nicole moves with youth to stay healthy. "Let's exercise, run, and jump so we can take care of our minds and bodies. Activity keeps us well. Our muscles and bodies grow when we play basketball or work together. It feels good to move and be exhausted from a good effort." Or, "Let's rest now. Reading or sitting quietly together will give us a chance to relax. Our minds and bodies need something more low-key. Let's stimulate our minds while our body rests. This will be good for our intellectual health and well-being."

Chores and Routines

Chores, routines, and self-care activities such as cleaning, eating, and dressing are not something to get through or over with but something to be in. Matt sweeps the floor with youth because this is something important to do together now. Nicole helps someone make his bed so they can talk while they do it. Meals are an excellent opportunity for eating, learning about food, and social interaction. A bedtime is an opportunity to talk and be together as youth transition to sleep.

The schedule of rituals and routines is fluid rather than rigid. Room is left to postpone a chore because the time is not right. They strive, in other words, for a balance between order and spontaneity. Matt makes a decision based on the tone and tempo of a moment to make beds later, delay dinner a few minutes, or to stick with the routine because the youth need a sense of order at the moment.

Struggle and Conflict

> We go crazy all night. Two fights, a few arguments, one runaway
> returned by police, a visit from a neighbor who thinks the kids
> stole his lawn mower, too many irrelevant phone calls, not enough
> food thawed for dinner, an angry mother, a depressed newcomer,
> and no breaks for us. Ronald and I struggle through . . . Gradually
> the house starts to fall silent. The radios play softly. There's a gig-
> gle and whisper. One by one the lights go out. It looks like we
> made it. (Desjardins & Freeman, 1991, p. 139)

Struggle and conflict are embraced as a central part of the dance.
When a conflict arises it is as an opportunity for learning. A youth gets
in Nicole's face and threatens to run away or hit someone. Nicole uses
her self (presence) to provide a sense of safety and security. Her message is, "I am here, aware of my feelings, and trying to understand the
events that contribute to your stress, anger, or sadness. My understanding, however, does not lessen my conviction to resolve this situation in a
peaceful way. Instead it increases my will to be firm and stand my
ground. I will not let you violate my space, run away, or hit. I understand your anger, sadness, and fear, but I will not let you express it in a
way that is harmful to others or me. My purpose is to help you settle
down and feel safe so we can talk about your feelings. I can see how angry or frightened or sad you are and, when the time is right, I want to hear
about your experience. We can work this out together."

Matt removes a youth from an activity and disciplines with sensitivity to the feelings that led to the youth's behavior and the impact of the
youth's behavior on others. His message is, "Your behavior is not ac-
ceptable, but you and your feelings are. I will welcome you back to our
activity and/or program when you can demonstrate that you are ready to
participate without hurting or infringing on the rights of others. We
might struggle, and our conflicts might not always be easily handled,
but we will try to work it through without rejecting each other. My goal
is to do it as safely and with as much understanding as possible. Whatever the result, we will try to use it as a learning experience."

Moments of Connection, Discovery, and Empowerment

During the preceding activities and while using all of these techniques, Matt and Nicole try to create as many moments of connection,
discovery, and empowerment as possible.

Moments of Connection: Matt sits quietly, talks, or walks to the store with the group engaged in walking and conversation. Nicole listens, looks, her attention focused on Maria. They are in synch, emotionally and physically, their feelings and movements more or less in harmony. Matt and Ron enjoy running together. As they move across the sidewalks, they share the same cadence.

Matt and Nicole rake leaves with all the youth, the pace and pleasure of their work in harmony. It feels good to be working together. The mood, tone, and space are just right. It is a human place of warmth and encouragement.

Nicole puts her hand on Nick's shoulder, slowly pulls it away, and says, "Let's go together." Nick walks alongside.

Moments of Discovery: A youth longs for closeness, but his feelings are compounded by new sexual feelings. Nicole and the youth discuss these feelings. The youth begins to understand that there are several ways to be close and that some of these ways are even more wonderful–and at the same time more frightening–than he previously imagined.

A boy is learning to improvise as he plays the piano. Each new chord combination seems to open the way for new possibilities. As he tests out these possibilities he also begins to refine his technique and recognize patterns of playing that run through his choices.

A boy depends on Matt and Nicole, yet he also wants to be free to do what he wants. Gradually the youth learns that dependence and independence are interconnected and that he needs both as he moves towards more independence. Or a girl has used her cognitive skills to work on a certain problem but then suddenly she becomes stuck. Nicole offers some hints on how to solve the problem. The girl is resistant at first but then takes some of the suggestions to heart and solves the problem using her internal cognitive skills, experience, and new information from the work to solve the problem.

In planning and moving through a day with youth, Matt orchestrates an activity or problem-solving exercise so a youth uses his current skills and abilities to develop new skills and abilities through interacting with her and/or the other youth. A girl, for example, is learning to play golf. She stands at the driving range next to another girl who already has a fairly good swing. The first girl knows the basic movements but is slicing the ball. The second girl shows the first girl how to adjust her grip and pull the club back. The first girl practices until she figures it out for herself.

A boy who has been rejected by a girl is sad and upset. Nicole talks with the boy about the first time she was rejected, suggesting that time and staying busy are helpful in dealing with feelings of loss. Gradually the boy learns to understand and cope with his feelings.

Moments of Empowerment: In a gymnastics activity Matt walks beside Ramon holding his hand as Ramon tries to traverse a balance beam. At first Ramon wobbles a bit using Matt's hand for support. After a few steps his confidence grows, and Matt lets go of his hand, realizing that if he moves a little faster he is less likely to lose his balance.

With the group Nicole works on several math problems, each problem based on using the same formula. They are fully engaged together in trying to solve the problems. She provides clues along the way and then they get it and begin to work alone on the problems. Maria, who has a fear of heights, climbs a hill with her. "That wasn't so bad," she says. Ron, who is afraid to ask a girl out for a date, talks with Matt and builds his courage, then calls the girl.

LEARNING TO DANCE

Matt and Nicole learn to dance through study and practice. They read books, listen, watch mentors, attend classes, practice, and innovate. As shall been seen in the next section of the volume, they get to know their own stories and how these stories shape the way they see the young people.

Imagine a classroom that is like a large dance hall: no chairs. Workers tell and listen to stories, sitting on the floor in a circle, then standing and critiquing each others' moves as they practice positioning, listening, creating boundaries, touching, mirroring.

Similarly, Matt, Nicole and the other Nexus youthworkers get to know and critique each other. "How well are we listening? Are we curious about one another? Where are we? How can we plan our learning together in a way that will welcome everyone to the learning process?"

Metaphors and analogies are used to enrich their discussions and learning. In addition to modern dance, they use metaphors and analogies such as a conversation or a game of basketball or a mealtime, exploring how their skills and attitudes can further their understanding of and competence in conducting their work.

The arts, philosophy, sociology, education, social work and other related fields provide new possibilities and ideas for their daily interactions with youth. Like many experienced practitioners, they realize there are more questions than answers and that being effective is largely a pursuit of the answers from a number of perspectives.

They share their learning and teach each other a technique by modeling it or by discussing a hypothetical case example. Learning is accented when they step back together, reflecting and analyzing a situation to see how it might be enhanced or repeated. They play with material.

Practice strengthens learning. In a conversation about learning youthwork, Henry Maier (see Maier, 1987, 1992, 1995) used the analogy of a child learning a summersault: "First we might demonstrate and talk about it, but it is not fully learned until the child does the summersault." Similarly, Matt, Nicole, the other workers, and youth do physical and mental summersaults until they get it.

Mistakes as well as successes inform their practice. In their quest to know and understand youthwork they remain open, learning from the whole of their experience: the yin and yang of a successful journey with youth. In preparation for their shifts, they stretch their minds and bodies, limbering up so they are free to be with youth. Like modern dances, they get their legs with experience. They learn how to line up and pass through, two basic techniques in dance. Nicole positions herself ("lines ups") with youth in the room–trying to use her body to mirror back what she sees. Matt (passes through) weaves through, in, and out of spaces.

While they weave in and out, they learn to read the story of their interactions. They use their natural instincts and train themselves to see and construct a story (the story of a shift or day, a youth's story, the story of an activity, their own story, etc.), to interpret it, play with it and get a feel for what it means.

They get their timing down–when to stand, sit down, move to the center, step to the side, raise or lower their voices or the light or music, and to quicken or slow the pace. Gradually, they learn, as Amy Evans says, to "show up" most of the time and, like the actor Willem Defoe, get out of their heads and into the movement. Together, they create unique human compositions, advancing the story and getting a feel for where they are in time and space in moments of connection, discovery, and empowerment.

SUMMARY

Natalie, the overnight worker, hears a sound in the bathroom. It's Maria, half asleep, getting a drink of water. Natalie stands silently in the doorway, smiling. After Maria puts her cup back on the shelf, Natalie walks behind her to the bedroom with both hands on Maria's shoulders, guides her to bed, and pulls the covers up to her chin. Maria yawns and falls back to sleep.

Nick's light is on. Natalie slowly opens the door. He's reading. "Are you okay?" she asks.

"I can't sleep."

"Want to talk?"

"No, thanks."

"I'm down the hall if you need me."

"Thanks."

Natalie checks on the other youth, all of whom are sound asleep, and goes back to the laundry room where she's folding some of their clothes and patching a hole or two.

"How did it go?" Rick and Karen ask Natalie, when they arrive for the morning shift.

"Okay, Maria got up for a drink and Nick couldn't sleep. He read for a couple hours. He's sleeping now."

They chat a while longer then Rick and Karen read the notes and begin to choreograph their next shift.

Chapter Two
Using Self and Story
to Understand Youthwork

Six youth–Isaac, Pat, Mary, Daniel, Carla, and Brunsey–and
I are in the woods, cross-country skiing through the southern Ket-
tle Moraine in Wisconsin. It is their first time. A moment ago, we
struggled to get their gear on. This section of the course is flat. I
demonstrate how to use the poles and how to glide, moving my
feet back and forth. It is a beautiful winter day.

"Boring," Brunsey says.

A group of young men with sleek outfits and equipment want
to pass. "Stay in the tracks to the right," I say. Stumbling, they
jump from one track to the other. The young men pass.

A few minutes later, we come upon a woman with her two
little daughters.

"Fuck!" Pat says as he catches a tip and falls.

"Watch your language." I give him a hand.

We pass the woman and her daughters. Pat, the strongest of
the group, powers ahead. Daniel and Carla ski side-by-side trying
to get more glide out of their skis. I fall behind a little and try to
give Mary, Brunsey, and Isaac a hand.

"I hate this shit," Isaac says, dusting off his butt.

"Wishbone your skis, dig in your edges, and keep your poles
behind you," I say as we approach the first major hill. It's a com-
edy of errors. For several minutes a stream of curses flow from

[Haworth co-indexing entry note]: "Using Self and Story to Understand Youthwork." Krueger, Mark.
Co-published simultaneously in *Child & Youth Services* (The Haworth Press, Inc.) Vol. 26, No. 1, 2004,
pp. 25-48; and: *Themes and Stories in Youthwork Practice* (ed: Mark Krueger) The Haworth Press, Inc., 2004,
pp. 25-48. Single or multiple copies of this article are available for a fee from The Haworth Document Delivery
Service [1-800-HAWORTH, 9:00 a.m. - 5:00 p.m. (EST). E-mail address: docdelivery@haworthpress.com].

Digital Object Identifier: 10.1300/J024v26n01_03

them as, one after another, they slip and fall backwards down the hill. At one point when Brunsey and Pat fall on top of me, we start laughing.

"Here, watch me." I demonstrate.

"I can do that." Daniel follows me up the hill.

Their arms ache as they dig their poles in behind them and try to keep themselves from slipping, but they all make it, then scream and holler as they speed down the other side.

Pat and Daniel are side-by-side now.

"I'll race you to the next hill," Daniel says.

Pat races ahead, muscling and grunting through the snow. Daniel uses technique to catch up and pass, but Pat lunges at the finish line.

"Who won?" he says, looking back with his face covered with snow.

"A tie," I say.

The sun begins to sink low in the sky. We make it around the course safely and then start a fire for the hot chocolate. Sitting on the logs shoulder-to-shoulder, we drink with our cold hands wrapped around the warm mugs.

For the past five years, I have participated with several youthworkers in a study of youthwork as an interpersonal process of interaction. Many of the themes defined previously were reaffirmed and others discovered during our inquiry.

Our inquiry includes four general steps. First, we try to be in our work fully so we can know and experience it. Second, we reflect on an experience. Third, we write a story about it. And fourth, as we write a story, we interpret it and look for themes and techniques that inform our practice.

While the differences are minimal, perhaps, what differentiates our process of inquiry from other forms of qualitative inquiry and reflective practice (Childress, 2000; Garfat, 1998; Moustakas, 1994; Nakkula & Ravitch, 1998; Van Manen, 1990) is the language of youthwork and the blending of what we have learned from our experience and the youthwork literature with what we have learned about story writing and qualitative inquiry. In short, we have tried to create a mix that feels right for understanding our work–a process of inquiry that is consistent with the way youthwork is experienced, practiced, and talked about.

Several youthworkers from a variety of programs have participated in our "research group"–some for short periods of times and others for several years. Amy Evans, John Korsmo, Joseph Stanley, Molly Weingrod, and Quinn Wilder have played major roles. Joseph has worked for several years in a shelter for runaway youth. Amy worked in the same shelter and now works in a counseling program. John and Quinn work with me at the university and are part-time youth mentors. John worked previously in community-based youth programs and Quinn in a residential treatment center. Molly, who has now gone on to the university, was a youth mentor (a youth mentoring youth) in the shelter. I was formerly a child and youth care worker in a residential program, and I am now a professor of youth-work. I serve as the facilitator.

Some of the experiences we write about are recent, and others are from the past. We meet every other week, usually in a small coffee house on the east side of Milwaukee or in a community agency. One or two workers serve as the primary reader. He or she will read a story and the rest of us will listen. After a story is read, we help each other rewrite and interpret the story while we simultaneously look for themes that run through and across the stories. During our discussions, the group also provides a source of support for the participants who enjoy talking about their work and being with others who have experienced similar struggles and successes.

Following is a story, "Take It Out," that I use to teach new team members:

> John, who is 15, takes a jump shot. The ball swishes through the net. "Twenty-two twenty-two," he says.
>
> "Twenty-four twenty-two, my favor," I say.
>
> "Bullshit, it's tied."
>
> "No it's not, I went four up with that hook shot," I say.
>
> We're playing one-on-one basketball in the rumpus room, a small gym in the basement of the treatment center. The basket is 8 feet high instead of the usual 10, making it possible for us to dunk the ball. It is hot. I open a window. Leaves have piled up against the metal grate. I take the ball and miss a shot. He grabs it, runs up the side of the wall, leans out over the basket and dunks the ball. "There asshole, now it's tied!"
>
> "Watch your language."
>
> We continue to play, the score going back and forth. I take the lead. He pushes me and goes up for a jump shot. I block it.
>
> "Fuck you!" John throws the ball against the wall, walks out of the room and slams the door behind him. I follow him up the stairs and out the main door. He sees me and runs down the hill be-

hind the treatment center toward the railroad tracks. I catch up in the woods before the tracks–an area frequented by hobos–and walk alongside.

We sit down, look at the tracks, and take a few breaths. The cool mist in the air feels good.

"Why did you get so upset?" I ask.

"You always have to win."

His comment catches me off guard.

"Don't you?" he says.

"I'm not sure. I guess I do . . . but I just can't let you win, can I?"

"That's just your excuse," he says.

I think another moment and then say, "Maybe you're right."

A train approaches. We get up, walk back together, and resume our game. I ease off a little. He takes the lead, then suddenly slams the ball against the wall again and shouts, "Don't let me win!"

INTERPRETATION

John and I brought separate experiences (meanings) to basketball. The skill level and nature of the activity gave us an opportunity to connect through doing something we both enjoyed, but it also created conflict. For me and, perhaps, him, the conflict was centered on our need to win and our competitive spirits, which I think we admired in each other.

I was confused. First, I knew that he could less afford to lose than I could. His prior life experiences were filled with failure and rejection. He was a good basketball player and an insightful youth, and he had had success in playing basketball and at school when he was able to keep himself under control, but he had also been severely abused by his father. There were many elements in this game that probably reminded him of his relationship with his father and drove John to beat him through beating me.

At the same time, I had learned that it was important to be real, genuine and sincere. And playing basketball at less than my capacity, at least at this point in my life, would not be genuine. I would be faking it, even if he would be aware that I was intentionally faking it. On the other hand, this might have been, as John suggested, my way of rationalizing my need to win. For him this also presented a conflict. He did not want to lose, but he did not want to win either if he knew I was not trying.

I am not sure that there is an single interpretation or conclusion to the challenge of this situation. Perhaps the answer is that an important aspect of child and youth care work is the paradoxical nature of this and other situations and that being aware of these paradoxes, rather than having the means to resolve them, is what is significant. In other words, John and I experienced life together as it was for us in those moments.

After that I began to increase the number of noncompetitive activities with John (jogging, painting, cooking, camping) and activities in which he excelled, such as gymnastics, and I also continued to play basketball with him. However, from that point on, I was never sure if I was playing at my full capacity. His words were always in the back of my mind.

Basketball is also a significant metaphor for me in understanding youthwork. Basketball, like child and youth care, has an ebb and flow. Moments of conflict are intertwined with moments of harmony. At times the game takes on a life of its own (the players get lost in the activity) and, at other times, the game seems like an obstacle.

Competence is the ability, I think, to be in these moments with a sense of understanding and presence. It might also be the ability to feel the rhythms of the game (child and youth care) and to intuitively move toward periods of "in synchness."

Following is a more detailed description of the procedures, practices, and beliefs that guide our inquiry along with additional stories and interpretations. As you will soon see, many of the skills we use in the study are the same as the skills we use in our practice, some of which were described in chapter one.

PREPARATION: MOMENTS FROM OUR YOUTH

An exercise we use to prepare and practice story writing is similar to a method used to counsel youth (Fay, 1989). This approach helps us unlock images in our mind that might enrich and/or bias our observations while we gain experience in story writing. We think of a moment from our youth–the first one that comes to mind. Then we sketch out this moment, building in what we saw, heard, felt, smelled, etc. "Sometimes, I can still remember the smell of my grandmother's coffee cake," I said recently, referring to this moment:

The tires crunch ahead of me on the frozen snow. I reach in the trunk and grab an armful of Sunday newspapers. My father drives slowly ahead. When I am cold, I sit inside next to him; the smell of his Old Spice aftershave fills the car. I walk from one house to another. The sun rises in the early morning sky. It feels like a warm washcloth on my face.

After all the papers are peddled, we stop at my grandmother's house. She is heavyset with ankle-less legs that seem to go straight into her shoes. With her eyes hidden behind her puffy cheeks and spectacles, I cannot tell if she is glad to see me or not but, as usual, the coffee cake is ready. Sometimes she has "pigs in blankets," but not today.

My father talks to her for awhile. I go into the unheated parlor where she keeps the Christmas tree until Easter. It is dark and dank except for a small sliver of light that shines beneath the door. Their voices are muffled.

"C'mon son, it's time to go," my father says with his voice raised.

On the way home, I hold the coffee cake in my lap. He reaches over, pinches my leg, and asks, "Everything copasetic, son?"

I don't know how to respond; I just pick at the crumbs.

Once we have written these moments we interpret them.

I liked being up early in the morning, doing something active and purposeful with the sun washing my face. I still do. In the fresh air, the world seems to open up with possibility.

I wanted to be like my father. At times, he seemed kind and strong. His aftershave was a symbol of being a man. I was also angry with him. He often stayed out late on Saturday nights at the bar as he had the night before. In hindsight, I think I wondered what kind of man I would be.

My grandmother, a stern German woman, was not very personable, but she always had that coffee cake. I wondered perhaps what it meant to be a loving person.

As they talked, I felt alone in the parlor. I didn't know how I felt when my father asked me. There was something inside: a mix of self-doubt, possibility, longing, perhaps.

These feelings undoubtedly influenced my work with youth. On some level, I think I related to their mix of emotions and their doubts about what they would become. I was also sensitive that their stories were full of very troubling moments that must have confused life even more for them.

Moments like these are important because they rise to our consciousness above millions of other moments from our youth and, thus, for one reason or another are key parts of our stories and the way we see the world. Throughout the course of our inquiry, we return to these moments to determine how they inform and bias our experiences and observations. Our goal is to not to become self-consumed with our histories but self-aware in a way that will open us to knowing our experiences and the youth's experiences.

BEING PRESENT

When we reflect on a moment and begin to write a story, we try to project ourselves into it (Nakkula & Ravitch, 1998). We want to be present ("show up" as Amy Evans says) so we can know and experience it again. As in our practice, this is perhaps the hardest part of the research. We have to constantly try to focus our energy and our actions on the moment. It is easy to get distracted or to read something into a moment or exclude something. It helps, as Joseph Stanley has taught us in many of his stories, to "deep breath" and "center" ourselves.

SELF AS INFORMANT

The self of the researcher is present throughout the process and, while understanding the phenomenon with increasing depth, the researcher also experiences growing self-awareness and self-knowledge . . . (Moustakas, 1994, pp. 9-11)

Throughout our inquiry (practice and reflection) we ask ourselves, "How does my experience influence what I see? How do my current feelings influence the way I interpret an interaction? How is/was my world different from the world of the youth? How is/was it the same? How does/did my presence influence the situation? What can I learn from my experience with others that will help me understand the true meaning of it?"

As depicted in the following story by Amy Evans, "Fear," our feelings inform us and open us to understanding a story.

I am walking into the inpatient unit of a hospital where a 10-year-old client of mine was admitted two days ago. The nurses' station is to my left, which I move toward. I can see people out of my right peripheral vision, and I am sure they are some of the kids staying on the unit. I feel a bit nervous, as this client of mine is quite defiant toward me.

I tell a couple of nurses behind the desk my first name and who I am to visit. They point to the table of kids I tried avoiding and say, "Lori, you have a visitor." I look in their direction and smile as I make eye contact with Lori and walk toward her.

They are playing UNO. Lori fans her cards up in front of her face and turns her head away from me and toward her peers. I'm thinking, "Oh great, here we go." I make brief eye contact with the other girls and say "hi" to them.

"Lori, can we go talk for a little bit together?"

"I don't know you–go away–I'm not talking to you."

"Maybe we can go talk in your room for a little bit."

The other girls are looking at Lori and at me. I smile a little bit at them and glance over at the nurses' desk when one of the nurses says, "Lori, go talk with your visitor; she is here to see you, go on." Lori stands up, throws her UNO cards down on the table and starts walking down the hallway. The nurse says, "Thank you, Lori."

I'm feeling almost invisible at this time. I follow Lori down the hallway. Upon arriving in her room she sits down on a bed. I'm unsure of what I should do.

"Does this bed belong to someone?"

"No." So I sit across from her on the other bed.

"I don't want you to come here. You embarrass me."

"Why do I embarrass you?"

"Because you are white coming in here talking to me."

I say, "That's okay, there are a lot of white people that work here and it is okay that I am white coming to visit you here."

Lori says she is allowed to cuss here on the unit and says some swear words. I try to make some small talk with her, and she answers using swear words. I smile to myself knowing I need not react, though I'm definitely feeling uncomfortable.

I start asking her about what brought her into the unit.

"Because I want to fuckin' kill myself and kill my fuckin' cousin."

We discuss this for awhile, and she is engaging enough with short answers and utilizing swear words to express herself.

"Let's do something. I'm bored."

"Do you want to play cards or color?"

"Color."

I get out my markers and ask her if she has paper. I'm glad she wants to do something, as this is consistent with our past sessions and her choice to engage with me for a longer period of time. She goes to her closet and retrieves some paper. She reads me a paragraph of a story she copied.

"That is a really good story and your printing looks so nice."

"No it doesn't. I write really ugly."

"No–it looks really good and nicely written."

Lori then takes the markers and starts drawing a picture. I continue talking with her about her situation and asking her things about it. She answers some things while coloring and continues swearing with her answers. I ask her if she needs to swear in order to talk, knowing that this would be completely unacceptable for her caregiver to allow her to swear. She says she "can fuckin' swear and I can even go tell."

Calmly, I say, "I'm not planning to go tell. I'm just wondering if you need to continue swearing for us to talk." She doesn't say anything and continues to color.

Lori then says she can draw on the wall and takes a green marker and draws a line on the wall. I smile again to myself at her rebellion/defiance.

"Okay, now you need to clean it off. You can lick your finger and it will come right off." I don't want her to worry that it won't come off.

She does this and then stops, "I don't have to lick my fuckin' finger; I can go get a paper towel."

"Okay."

She gets off the bed and goes to her bathroom and brings back a wet paper towel. She cleans off the green line. She then takes a black marker and writes her name on the wall.

"Now you need to clean that off too and not write on the wall anymore."

She cleans off her name and sits back on the bed and looks at me.

I bring up an issue that occurred in school the day she was admitted as an inpatient.

"Does it look like I am at school, you motherfucker?"

"No. I would like to talk about what happened that day at school."

"Does it look like I am at school, you motherfucker?"

"No. I would like to talk about what upset you with the principal that day."

"Do you see the principal here, motherfucker?"

"What made you upset with him that day?"

"Do you see the principal here, motherfucker?"

"You know I want to stay here with you and talk with you and I care about you, but I'm not going to stay since it seems like you don't want to talk."

I'm feeling confident and defeated at the same time. I put on my jacket.

"Okay, okay." (Like she often says when given an ultimatum to change her behavior.)

"No, I'm going to go now and I will come back and visit you a different time."

"Take it easy. I'll talk to you soon."

I walk out the door.

"I hate you."

I walk toward the nurses' station where I wait for a minute, wishing they would hurry up and let me out, but they are busy. I cannot leave until they unlock the unit door. Before any nurses notice me, Lori comes out of her bedroom and states loudly, "You forgot your marker, Amy." I think, "Oh good, she is reaching out to connect." And I'm feeling also somewhat nervous about her unpredictability.

"Okay." I start walking toward her room.

"I will get them." She runs ahead.

I wonder if she does or does not want me to come back down to her room. As she comes back into the hallway with the markers, I am almost to her room. She reaches the markers to me.

"Do you want to talk now?"

"Okay." We go back into her room.

Our time together that followed was not smooth and easy, of course, but she did talk more about her situation and, when asked if she wanted me to visit her on the unit next week if she is still here, she says, "Yes." (I'm thinking she means this at least on some level, and it will most likely be the same walls next week at least much of the session.) I ask Lori if she would like to walk me to the door.

"Okay." She walks me back to the nurses' station before she turns back and heads off to a group that is in session.

"See you later, Lori," I say as she walks back down the hall.

HEARING AND SEEING

As in our practice, reflections, and story writing, we try to hear and see what goes on around us. Amy writes, "The nurses' station is to my left, which I motion toward. I can see people out of my right peripheral vision and I'm sure they are some of the kids staying on the unit."

We also try to sort through the multitude of sounds and sights to focus on what is in need of attention–eyes and ears focused on the specific as well as the general–as Amy did and John Korsmo does in his story, "Tony."

I see a boy looking through the screen door as I approach the house. The main door is open despite the frigid February day. He sees me coming up the walk.

"He's here! He's coming."

I climb the four steep steps to the porch and feel heat coming from the house. I knock and a woman comes and opens the screen door, without looking at me.

"Come on in. Sorry for the mess."

She is wearing cut-off sweat pants and a tank top. The boy who was watching for me through the screen is wearing boxer shorts and no shirt. He's sitting on a couch, chewing on the edge of a pillow he has in his lap. I kick all the snow off my shoes and step into the house. She lets the door swing shut and sits on the couch next to her youngest son.

She motions to a chair across from her. "Have a seat. I'm not sure where he's at. Upstairs, I think. I know he knows your comin' though. I made him get up this mornin' and didn't let him leave 'cuz he woulda just took off 'n not showed up when you came."

I introduce myself to her, take off my coat, and sit down on the chair. It is so warm in the house I feel like I am going to break into a sweat. I can hear someone on the stairs, and the mother yells, "Tony, come here and sit your ass down."

We make eye contact as he turns the corner and heads for a chair against the wall. Like his brother, he is wearing only boxers and no shirt. He is 14 years old, but he could easily pass for 9 or 10. I introduce myself to him, start a bit of small talk, and fill him in about what he can expect of me as his new mentor.

I'm starting to ask some questions about his interests and hobbies, when his mother interrupts. "You ain't queer, are ya?"

Both boys snicker.

"No, in fact I just got married last summer. Maybe you'll meet my wife one of these days."

"I ain't tryin' to be funny, but you never know these days, and I ain't gonna' send him off with just nobody. You can see he ain't so big yet. He's smart enough 'n all, but I don't think his body's matured yet. Look at him. Raise up your arm and show the man. He ain't even got hair yet. I don't know about down there." She motions to his lap. "I ain't gonna' look, but I know he ain't got no hair in his armpits."

"Shut the fuck up." His high voice emphasizes his small frame and clashes with his language.

"Don't fuckin' talk to me like that. Show him. Raise your arm up 'n show the man."

"You know, it doesn't matter to me if he has hair under his arms or not." I glance over at him, and I'm surprised that he has both arms up in the air like he's getting ready for a stick-up, to show me his hairless underarms.

She points to him. "See what I mean?"

"So what?" he screams back at her as he puts his arms down.

We talk for a few minutes about how everyone grows at different rates. I assure her that he's not the only 14-year-old boy without hair under his arms.

After a few minutes I suggest that Tony and I go outside. "Want to go to the park?"

He jumps up. "I'll go to put some clothes on."

While he is upstairs putting on his clothes I tell his mom that I respect her questions about my background and about my sexuality. We discuss some of the fears she has that something could happen to one of her boys.

Tony comes back down with some clothes on. We head across the street to a park, and I breathe in some crisp air to cool myself down.

"It feels kind of nice out here, doesn't it?"

"Yeah, it's hot as hell in there. She always does that when she knows somebody's coming over. Cranks the fuckin' heat up so you can't even sleep."

"Yeah, it's pretty warm in there alright."

He laughs and kicks a dead, frozen bird that is in his walking path. The bird skates across the crunchy snow and stops by a cracked plastic baseball that is buried halfway under the snow. We toss the ball back and forth for a few minutes. Tony spots a stick that will work for a bat, and we take turns pitching and batting. He bats ten times, and then I bat ten times. We talk about school and his home while we play. It's his turn at bat, and he's predicting a homer.

I bend over to tie my shoe and, before standing back up, I make a quick snowball. He is ready to crush the ball out of our make-believe stadium, so I wind up for a fast underhand pitch. He swings the bat before realizing I pitched a snowball and not the plastic baseball. He makes good contact and snow sprays all over both of us.

"Oh, shit," he yells, and we laugh and wipe snow off our faces before he retaliates, and we launch into a playful snowball fight, chasing each other around the park until we're both wet and winded and red from the cold.

"You got me, man. That was a good one," he says. "I didn't even see you make that snowball. I was going to kill that pitch, too." We laugh some more and start walking towards his house, both of us rubbing our hands and blowing on our fingers.

AWARENESS OF THE MEANING OF ACTION

Words alone do not tell a story. When a youth "is in another youth's face," what appears to be the start of a fight might instead be part of a street ritual that is a competition of wit rather than fists. When a youth and a youthworker are jogging together and laughing, the shared rhythm lends to the formation of their connection in the moment (Maier, 1992). A smile might be an expression of joy or a cover for fear or uncertainty. Sometimes nothing is more telling than a sigh, smile, or an action such as a youth getting up from his chair and joining an activity, or a closed fist as in the following story, "Experiments in Silence," by Molly Weingrod.

We were not used to having younger kids around the house. And working with 11-year-olds is very different than working with 16- and 17-year-olds. Those several years in-between are longer than any others. And trying to get a whole group composed of both ages to sit and focus on one thing was impossible. Even asking them to cut out pictures from magazines and paste them in other places was way too demanding. One 11-year-old was trying to irritate everyone, and the other 11-year-old irritated everyone without trying. The 15-year-old, Nathan, didn't speak very good English, which automatically made him the target for all the distraction. "Hey man, say elephant," or "say dollar," or "teach me a Spanish word besides 'buta.'"

He finally realized everyone was laughing at him more than with him and started mumbling words he knew they'd understand: "Shut up, man," and "Fuck you." I told him he could go in the back room to finish his artwork in silence. He did–or tried. Sporadically, kids tried to follow him back there and engage him or would yell things to him through the walls. The group had begun without cohesion and was growing into disaster, words becoming more aggressive by the moment. And the artwork only complicated things more. We stumbled through the full hour, hoping we would not lose it, but knowing too that we already had.

When we finally admitted it was over and began cleaning up, most everyone was gone from the table, already needing movement. I went into the back room where Nathan had been working and found him surrounded by "hyped kids," flying foosballs, and too many conversations. He was sitting at the piano but with his back to it, leaning his chair on only the back legs, his head covered with his sweaty, gray sweatshirt. I leaned against the piano and saw his hand, hanging off to the side of the chair, balled up into a resilient fist, and hard. I stared at it for a moment, maybe amazed at the intensity it radiated, trying to pry it open with my eyes like the girl on the TV show, *Bewitched*. But it stayed closed and silent. I said his name a few times, and when I asked him what was going on, he took his shirt from his head but remained silent. I told him he could go in the front room and close the door if he wanted to get away from everybody. But he shook his head. I asked if he wanted to go for a walk, and he lifted his shoulders and eyebrows, quietly saying, "I don't know." I waited a minute and then said "Come on, let's go take a walk." I got up and he followed me.

I stopped to tell the supervisor we'd be back soon. Nathan walked out the door and, walking behind him, I watched his fist, still glowing with anger and tightly closed. He waited for me in the alley, and we walked side by side for four blocks without saying a word–only breathing and lost in our own thoughts and footsteps.

We never looked at each other either. I only saw his t-shirt swinging over his shoulder with his walk, out of the corner of my eye. When we got back to the house, I opened the door and he walked past me. I looked at his hands and, though still closed, there was a space, room for some breathing, calmed, beginning to open.

OPEN-ENDED STORIES

Most of the stories in youthwork, like "The Race," by Quinn Wilder, are open-ended. They do not have neat plots or tidy beginnings and endings but are comprised of interactions that occur in moments and continue to influence the larger evolving stories of an individual or event.

It is late fall or early winter, and I park the car on the road a few blocks from the museum. We've been together now for about 2 months, 15 hours per week. I feel like we're hitting a groove. I've got him willing to go to the museum, since we've exhausted all the other possibilities we can think of and agree upon. Or maybe it is that our relationship has developed to the point where what we do together matters less than just being together doing something, anything.

The air coming off the lake is really cold, and we hesitate before getting out of the car. He's telling me about the things his parents do that bug him.

I say something to him about how he should try to listen to his parents more.

He stops my lecture with, "You know, you're just like my parents. You're not funny; you're not like my friends. I don't know why I'm even here with you. This is stupid." He slams the door, standing in the street as he says this, looking down at the ground.

I stop feeding the parking meter and look at him.

"Well, you're right, I'm not like your friends. I'm older, for one thing. But we can still have fun–"

"No, we don't, this is stupid. I don't know if I'm gonna' do this mentoring thing anymore."

We start walking towards the museum. In front of the museum, there is a water fountain with a statue of an unclothed boy, eternally peeing into the pool below. I know that Dylan is planning on pointing it out when we get there, probably thinking that I will be embarrassed by it or at least that I will frown upon his pointing it out.

I am thinking about his comments. "Not funny?" I'm funny, at least I can be, and I can be fun to be with. But I have been harping on him a lot, lecturing him, because a couple weeks ago the social worker and the parents asked me to more strictly enforce some behavioral goals with him and to make our activities together more structured and purposeful. And I have been. But it is obviously just more of the same for him, and I think as a mentor I should be taking a different approach than the other adults in his life are taking with him. He's right; I haven't been any fun.

"Look, Dylan, I don't want to be that way all the time. We should have fun together, right? From now on, we're just having fun, Okay?"

"Yeah, whatever."

I feel the need to do something goofy to re-set the tone, so I can start really having fun. Then it occurs to me. We're still a block away from that statue at the front of the museum.

"Race you to the penis," I say, and I take off running, leaving Dylan temporarily stunned, laughing too hard to really run. He's howling as he catches up to me at the base of the statue, repeating, "I can't believe you said that!"

We walk into the museum together.

SPEAKING ACROSS THE SPACES OF OUR EXPERIENCES

To understand the meanings of our stories, we speak (in our heads and conversations) across the spaces of our experiences (Garfat, 1998; Moustakas, 1994; Saleebey, 1994; Sarris, 1993; Vander Ven, 1999a). We search for a mutual reality (make meaning) with the awareness that everyone has a unique story that determines how he or she sees and makes meaning of the world (Bruner, 1990). We ask ourselves and others, "How do/did or might you have seen it? What is/might it be like from another perspective?" If a story is being constructed as it is occurring, we might ask a youth or a colleague what they experienced, or we might go back later and ask. At the very least we try to understand what it might have been like from someone else's perspective based on our knowledge of that person.

NOTE TAKING, SKETCHING

Like James Joyce, Jack Kerouac, and the stream-of-consciousness Beat writers, we do not want to mess with the subconscious. As we write notes in our heads and on paper, our goal is to let the experience come out freely. We try to capture the immediacy of the moment and let the dialogue and action carry the moment. Then gradually we shape our notes into a story, as shall be seen a little later.

Each of us goes about note taking differently. Some of us have extensive written notes while others keep most of the notes in their head or begin writing a story as a form of note taking. In his notes Joseph Stanley writes:

> Youth called: "Hello!!!" . . . I told my mother that I got kicked out of summer school–"I'm proud that you did that!!!"–"She's pissed."–"What would happen if you apologized?"–"Nothing." Silence Silence–"I'll try"–"Hold on." Five minutes pass. "She's better I guess."–"I'm proud."–"You took a chance . . . also, I'll see you tomorrow . . . thanks for the call . . . I'm proud"–"Thanks"–"Yeah"–"Bye."

Joe, an experienced worker, who is perhaps the most Kerouac-like among us, leaves his stories pretty much the way they come out in these notes. Unlike Joe, however, most of us work and rework and add and subtract to our initial sketches.

WRITING WITH ACCURACY AND KNOWING

With the notes as a guide, several drafts of each story are written. It is a bit like sculpting with clay. We work the clay until the shape within reveals itself. Material is cut out and put back in and cut out until it appears and feels right. We ask ourselves, "Is this consistent with the way the situation presented itself?" After we read our stories, reflect, and listen to our colleagues' comments, we rework the story.

In quoting the poet Ezra Pound, short story writer Raymond Carver (1983) wrote, "Fundamental accuracy of statement is the sole morality of writing" (p. 21). Similarly, we want each sentence and word to be accurate so that our story describes as nonjudgmentally as possible a situation as it actually was. Is this really exactly how I said or hear it? As mentioned a moment ago, if it is a recent experience, we might go back and ask a youth or colleague if they experienced the moment the same way we did. The only things we intentionally change are the names and some of the details that might identify a specific youth.

A frequent comment in our conversations is, "Let the action and dialogue move the story forward." Our tendency is to want to explain and analyze too much as we are writing the story, and explanation and analysis should only enter a story if that is what we were doing in our conversation or heads at the time. It helps some of us to write in the present tense, because that makes us think about how the story occurred in the moment.

Writing is also a way of knowing–a method of discovery and analysis (Richardson, 2000, p. 923; Van Manen, 1990). We learn more about ourselves and our subject as we write about it. Each new draft is a discovery that takes us closer to the truth.

PAUSES, TEMPO, MOVEMENT

To get our story to look, feel, and sound right we try to replicate the pauses and tempo of an experience. Reading a story out loud often alerts us to when we are off. The words might be correct, but the story does not sound or feel right as spoken. When this happens, we try to listen to ourselves and go back to the drawing board until it reads correctly, as Joseph Stanley tries to do in a story about a moment of anger and frustration:

> It's Sunday–Sleepy eyed–Relax–Catch up on paperwork-day. A presence flashes through the door. Through sleepy eyes I respond–"It's good to see you." Slight pause–though my eyes are limited at the moment–I feel his stare. I respond–"You don't look good." "Hmm-hmm–I, hmm, haven't been sleeping." I feel sharp breaths–sharp jabs–from his presence. "You look-much worse then that." "Hmm-yeah-hmm–I'm depressed–I hmmh–Sad." I try to take some deep breaths–"What have you been doing?" "I'm bored!" Thoughts flood me ("When are you going to take responsibility?"–screams in my head). I feel angry–minutes flood by–breathe/relax–I let silence steal the moment–to rule the moment–taking in long slow-deep breaths–exhaling even slower.

"What do you mean by depressed–hmm?"–is all he shares. You look really unkempt today–you're not taking care of yourself–I feel my own anger well up–breathe. I'm depressed–tumbles out of him–not really share so much by speech. Anger–I grasp the silence–focus on breathing–taking in deep breaths–exhaling–I slowly while breathing focus on a clearing–in the middle of the woods–the sun shines brightly while in the background I hear the waterfall.

What are we going to do about it? I don't know is shared as a sharp knife. Let's look at what we can do. I don't know flows out even sharper–it feels painful. You can? I raise my arms–while taking in deep breaths of air. Breathing I focus on flowing calm water–and the bright sun on my face. Silence-silence-silence-hmm-more silence-silence. I don't know sharply enters the air. Silence–briefly I concentrate on taking in deep breaths. Call my mother–quietly breaks the air. About? Silence-silence-silence-silence-breathe-silence. Will you call her, hmm, to talk about it?

INTERPRETATION

As a story is sculpted, we ask, "Why did he or she behave this way? How do they (I) feel? What led to these feelings? How did our interactions influence the outcome? What did it mean?" During this process we, in a sense, break the story down to try to get at the essence of what occurred. We want to know what is essential to know about that moment to enrich our understanding.

We help each other. "Have you considered this or that? It seems to me that one way to look at it is this way. In my experience of a similar event, I saw it as different. I think it needs more dialogue, because I got lost in the middle. Yes, that rings true with my experience and what others seem to say about their experience," giving our colleague alternative considerations and/or affirmation to help him or her find the true subjective/objective meaning of his or her experience, as Molly Weingrod did in her interpretation of "Experiments in Silence."

While we were walking, the first few minutes were uncomfortable for me. I wanted to say something or thought I should, but when I tried nothing would come out. There was something inside me fighting for silence. At that point I realized nothing I said or asked would resolve anything for him. In this case words would only soothe my discomfort with the situation. I spent the rest of the walk picturing his tight fist and imagining it open, calmed.

Upon reflection, my silence had done two things for Nathan. It allowed him to be angry. But I gave him space to be angry in so that building vertically on itself the anger could spread out everywhere and eventually be buried by stronger powers of time and space. Also, my silence allowed him to experience and feel something harmful and to share it with someone. By not saying anything, I was letting him know that it was okay with me that he was angry and that I wasn't going to try to change him. Earlier, was obvious to me that Nathan *wanted* to be angry. I was willing to share it with him but not to solve anything (which I couldn't do anyway). He wanted to feel powerful and strong by making a fist, but I allowed him to feel powerful by knowing that he could deal with his anger on his own, by not giving any of my input.

Silence can become a manipulative tool when one person is speaking and needing a response, and the other refuses to speak. But in this moment, silence served as an equalizer. Earlier, Nathan had refused to speak, so then I made the same choice as he did and stayed silent–not even looking at him while we were walking–not waiting for him to break. Sometimes someone wants to be alone but wants to be alone with someone else. We each were alone in that moment together.

Amy Evans interprets "Fear":

It seems that Lori doesn't really understand her world and who is in it and does not try to trust in people around her. Although Lori does want relationships. It might be kind of like fate that our paths have crossed as we both can learn a lot from each other. And if this did not occur I don't believe that either of us would choose to continue to interact with one another. It is painful. I also believe that fear is part of our interactions in what may be discovered/revealed about ourselves.

Within our interactions, even though painful, I feel acceptance of her but not acceptance of her pain. I believe she knows that I will not abandon her. Also, in terms of the dialogue regarding Lori feeling embarrassed about myself being white, I do feel race and cultural differences are extremely important. My response to her statement is one of not reacting, because she attempts often to get reactions out of me. She did not raise the issue again so I believe that she was looking for a conflict at that moment, and/or it wasn't one of the most important issues she felt at the time.

In the interpretation of his story, "The Race," Quinn Wilder writes:

This story has lots of themes for me. The one that stands out the most is the balancing act the youthworker plays between being the fun, peer-like friend and being the "adult" with expectations, or at least enforcer of other adults' expectations. I needed and wanted our time together to really be fun most of the time. He had to want to have a relationship with me for it to work at all. I believed that the behavioral issues he was having at home and school would become less of a problem for him if we had an ongoing, mutually respecting friendship. But at the same time, the treatment team professionals and the parents wanted to know that I was enforcing their messages. I had to have faith that youthwork would work, and I had to convince others who didn't have that faith.

On another level, this story is about "turning the mood." In just one minute, it went from miserable complaining to pure joy. How do we construct these turnarounds, and how do we know when they are called for? I had to honestly reflect upon what Dylan was saying, admit he had a point, and then figure out what to do about it and finally pull it off. It's not easy, and I'm sure I've failed to do this many times, but I think that "turning the mood" is probably a frequently occurring challenge for many youthworkers.

John Korsmo interprets "Tony" as follows:

There were a number of things going on in this short visit with Tony and his family. This was my first visit with them after a very brief telephone conversation with his mom, setting up the appointment. I was assigned to Tony as a paid mentor through a juvenile offender's program. I had a feeling that this family had some previous experience with people being assigned to come to their home before for one reason or another.

The heat inside the house and the way it looked, as though someone had quickly straightened things up with stuff stacked against the walls and piled in corners and hidden behind furniture, reminded me that I was a symbol of "the system." In fact, it reminded me very much of a time when I was about 12 years old and a social worker came to meet my parents and me. The moment I stepped into their overheated house I thought of the unlucky young social worker who was assigned my family and me more than 20 years ago. I remembered stoking the wood stove to prove we were capable of keeping heat in the house. I remembered my mom apologizing about the dirty house, despite my 20-minute, feeble attempt to hide the messes that had taken months to accumulate. I tried to shake the memory for a bit so I could focus on Tony and his mom.

I was caught off-guard when Tony's mom asked if I was queer. Not because of the intimacy of the question or even the crass way she asked, but because I had met with so many families recently who did not ask a thing about me, parents who simply handed their kids over to me as if I was a valet parking a run-down car. I answered her honestly and tried to let her know that I was pleased with her interest in knowing more about my qualifications for taking her child out of her house.

I was consciously trying not to pass judgment about this woman's intellect or lack thereof but was disturbed by the way she spoke with and about her children and particularly when she referenced his lack of pubic hair and general slow development. I was not surprised at all when Tony told his mom to "fuck off," although I was surprised that he obeyed her demand to show me his underarms. While Tony was getting dressed I talked to his mom about adolescent development and different rates of growth and about some of the emotions and behaviors that often accompany puberty and "coming of age." She acted interested, but my interpretation was that she was mostly concerned that he was going to be picked on or harassed for not being a real man, even though he was only 14.

I suggested going to the park for as many selfish reasons as any else. I was sweating in the house and was quite uncomfortable and knew that we would not have much of an opportunity to connect in there. But, mostly, I just needed to get outside and be away from her negativity for a moment. The fresh air and freedom of the wide-open park proved to be a good medicine for both Tony and me.

As we left the heat and rank smell of the house, we hit it off right away. We had no real plan but went with the flow of the moment and talked and played and had a good time together. We laughed and joked around and teased each other in a way that I think made both of us comfortable. I could empathize with Tony and I think he felt that I understood him. Despite the rocky start in the house, this was a very positive beginning of a relationship for the two of us.

Joseph Stanley interprets an untitled moment:

> Theme, youth seemed to need my support to carry out his intent. Just being there–presence is enough. There are always positives to recognize. Also my experience and book knowledge support the concept that a positive nurturing adult increases resiliency in youth who come from problematic childhood.

THEMATIC ANALYSIS

As we listen to and read through the stories, our own and our colleagues, we look with intensity at the inter-relatedness of micro and macro events and the truth or reality that is created with the addition of feeling and intuitive thought (Bruner, 1990), simultaneously interacting, feeling, experiencing, observing, and looking back.

In what he defines as entering into self-dialogue, Moustakas (1990, p. 16) argues that to know a phenomenon one has to engage in a rhythmic flow with it, moving back and forth again and again until multiple meanings are discovered. To understand the wholeness and unique patterns of experience (Fewster, 1990; Moustakas, 1990), we often move from specific to general and back again. Quoting Craig (1978), Moustakas (1990) wrote, "From the feeling to the word and back to the feeling; from the experience to the concept and back to the experience" (Craig, 1978, p. 57).

Sometimes it is as if we are looking through a kaleidoscope. Patterns or insights often emerge as we sift and sort through the data (stories of observations, feelings, and experiences). We sense how a youth feels based on previous experience. Or we interact with the material (thoughts, observations, notes, and experiences) and mold it. We try to become part of the process, changing and being sensitive to how these changes influence the meaning of our interactions.

Comments are also solicited from other participants in the study and outside experts. For instance, the researcher might ask a youth or another worker, "In these moments were these themes present?" Or people who were not involved but who have expertise in youthwork or related human service fields might be asked to take an unbiased look at the workers' stories to shed light on similar or additional themes. Finally, we compare the thematic findings to the literature, asking, "Is this confirmed by history and/or what other workers experience?"

INFORMED PRACTICE

Our practice is informed throughout our inquiry as we write, interpret, and talk about our stories. Thus far we have also identified several themes that run through several stories. Most of the themes are not new. They have been written about before in youthwork and/or in related fields. What is new is the context and the sense of the affirmed and additional importance that is placed on a theme. For example, *silence* emerged as an important theme when it appeared in several stories. This has taught us to pay more attention to when it is time to speak and when it is better to just be quiet, such as in Molly's ending to "Experiments in Silence" and Joe Stanley's untitled moment. It has also taught us to value the pauses and to enjoy silence as a meaningful part of the work.

Presence, in addition to a method of inquiry, was also at the center of many stories. Being in the moment is undoubtedly central to effective youthwork practice as well as research. Our stories show how we can be present in different contexts and, in particular, the importance of breathing, as Amy Evans writes in her interpretation of "showing up."

At the beginning of the study we knew that *transitions* were an important part of our work. The study not only affirmed this but also suggested that transitions were an even bigger part than we thought. And again, our stories gave us several new contexts within which to understand transitions.

Fear and/or *self-doubt* are continuous themes. We are often anxious or afraid of how we might react or how someone else will act. Our work is risky, and understanding and accepting fear is central to our success.

In a recent conversation we talked about how much of the work is not about resolution. Things do not always work out or come to a neat ending. In many moments we are frustrated, bored, struggling, angry. And in other moments we are there, just being. The key is–no matter what is occurring–to be there.

SUMMARY

We write and interpret stories about daily interactions and look for themes that help inform us about our practice. The goal is to "be in" youthwork and then shape and work a story until it captures the essence of a moment or interaction and to learn from the story and the themes in several stories. This circular process of constructing and deconstructing stories, searching for themes, and writing new stories continues as we delve deeper and deeper into the meaning of our experiences in youthwork.

Chapter Three
Moments with Youth

Following are additional stories and interpretations by John Korsmo, Molly Weingrod, Joseph Stanley, Quinn Wilder, Amy Evans, Rick Flowers, Arcelia Martinez, and Pam Ramsey. The stories and interpretations are presented as teachable moments that are examples of how we are learning to understand youthwork and, as such, are open to further interpretation and learning by the readers. Each worker has also included a personal sketch.

JOHN KORSMO

Meandering the shore of a stormy ocean is one of my favorite things to do: bending to touch and investigate as many things as may pique my interest, passing judgment on what will land in my bag and what will get tossed back down. I pick out unique shells, rocks, and glass, oddly forced and molded pieces of wood, and occasional man-made objects that have drifted ashore, aware of the complete power of the unpredictable water beside me. I'm aware that with every step I may be burying a shell or stone that is even more brilliant than the one I have in my hand, or that on any occasion if only I would have concentrated to the right or to the left or just an inch beyond the scope of my immediate vision I could have stumbled upon something magnificent.

The unpredictability and power of the ocean is an appropriate metaphor for my boyhood in a family weathered and beaten by alcoholism,

---

[Haworth co-indexing entry note]: "Moments with Youth." Krueger, Mark. Co-published simultaneously in *Child & Youth Services* (The Haworth Press, Inc.) Vol. 26, No. 1, 2004, pp. 49-76; and: *Themes and Stories in Youthwork Practice* (ed: Mark Krueger) The Haworth Press, Inc., 2004, pp. 49-76. Single or multiple copies of this article are available for a fee from The Haworth Document Delivery Service [1-800-HAWORTH, 9:00 a.m. - 5:00 p.m. (EST). E-mail address: docdelivery@haworthpress.com].

abuse, and poverty. Such beachcombing is how I have become the person I am, combing life for things, people, and experiences of excitement and interest, knowing full well that with every choice I make there are a million castoffs.

It is also the way I engage with youth, paying attention to what is "in hand" knowing all the while there may be something profound only inches or moments away and respecting the significance and the unpredictability of the controlling powers off to the side (parents, peers, systems, etc.).

Boss

He's shooting pool as is his usual after-school routine. I'm happy to see him and start to walk over. Watching him I remember last summer when he asked me if he could start a pool league for the center's younger kids.

Then one day he bought a billiards rulebook with his own money, and the league took off from there. We decided he could be called the commissioner. He wrote "Commissioner" after his name on all of the flyers he posted all over the place.

I gave him a clipboard, and he wrote "POOL LEAGUE–DON'T TOUCH" on it in big red letters. He came to the center every day with a lesson plan written out on lined notebook paper and clipped to the board. He brought his own red binder and created an attendance sheet that I copied after each practice and each tournament. He kept them in the binder and took the binder home with him each night.

One day he showed up with a 10-question test for the kids to take, and he let them know that the only way they would get a certificate of completion was if they passed each test. They had to get 7 out of the 10 questions right in order to pass.

He is a big, solid kid. He has bright red hair, fair skin, and huge freckles on his face, neck, and arms and is one of only a few white kids who come to the center. At least six feet tall and well over 200 pounds, he has thick rolling shoulders, and his left forearm and bicep are huge. His right arm is lame and dangles, half cocked, from his thick shoulder. His pointer finger on that hand sticks out pretty much straight in the air, but his other three fingers are tightly curled up toward his bent, limp thumb. He has a pronounced limp protecting a weak right leg and hip flexor.

He takes his time as he lines up for a one-handed bank shot. Kids walk by and poke him or smack the cue.

"It's a cue, not a stick, Johnny." He always calls me Johnny when he's trying to make a point.

I have known him for a couple years and have been, at times, impressed with his patience and tolerance of harassment from other kids, but at other times I am frightened by his ability to snap without warning. The harshness and power he exudes send a bit of tension through the entire center.

He does not realize how strong he really is. I talk to him frequently about not touching other kids, because he squeezes too hard and hurts them. We talk a lot about options for dealing with feelings and anger, including alternatives to breaking pool cues and throwing people to the ground.

Today he is letting kids get away with their free pot shots at him, answering with a sideways half-grin and a nod, "What's up?"

I wait for him to make his shot before approaching to say hello. His mouth is moving and I'm sure he's calling his shot to himself. He draws back and strokes forward, the cue hitting the ball with a thud that was clearly a bad shot.

"Fuckin' ball."

"It wasn't the ball's fault."

He turns around and smiles, limping over me to give me a hug.

He's called "Red" by most of the kids in the center on account of his thick, shiny red hair, but we call each other Boss. He reminds me of Steinbeck's Lenny from *Of Mice and Men*. We joke around a lot and I go into my Lenny impersonation when he squeezes me from the side for a one-armed hug that makes me feel like my ribs could crack.

"Oh, come on, Boss. Let me pet the rabbits."

We both laugh and he lets up his grip.

"I won't hurt the rabbits, Boss," he tells me, and then giggles like mad, turning back towards the table.

"Where you been, Johnny?"

He always asks me where I have been even though he just saw me yesterday.

Interpretation

The entire moment in "Boss" took place within a 3-minute time frame. I had just returned back to the center from a meeting and was making the rounds to check on the place–to see who was there and what was going on. As indicated in the story, we had a positive relationship, and I believe I was one of only a handful of people who he felt respected by and attached to.

Like so many moments with youth, there are several themes or points of interest that could be picked out of this one. While the reader can determine them for him or herself, a few that came to my mind as I wrote it were:

- ritualistic/predictable behavior;
- we saw each other every day and had a similar conversation each time;
- Red's methodical way of playing pool and of communicating;
- the predictable manner in which Red was treated by the other kids and myself;
- sense of mastery/importance;
- Red was proud of his ability to play pool and of his "position" running the league for the younger kids;
- I acknowledged Red for his abilities and accomplishments and encouraged him to take a leadership role (although he initiated it);
- sense of being needed;
- it was very important for Red to be the coach and to be needed by the younger kids;
- it was equally important for Red to understand how much I counted on him to fulfill his volunteer duties (I was clear with him from the outset that I expected him to complete the league if he started it and regularly communicated with him about appreciating his accountability);
- humor/lightheartedness/fun;
- we laughed together every day;
- we had fun together and made sure fun was a key component of his pool league;
- positive relationship and understanding;
- we understood each other's needs and expectations (for instance, Red knew I did not want to hear profanity in the center. I did not need to scold him or otherwise discipline him for his use of bad language too much–I simply needed to let him know I heard it–and remind him to be aware of it)

Similarly, there are several points of the story that could send up red flags to some, including the affection, my allowing Red to run a program at the center (as a youth, himself), our reference to Lenny and Boss (given Red's physical and mental similarities to Lenny and how it could be misconstrued as my being mean or demeaning), the soft responses to profanity and confrontation. I encourage readers to consider their own interpretations of the dynamics of the relationship and what was going on in the story and to consider what seems to have been working, for whom, and why.

MOLLY WEINGROD

At 18 I have no degrees, little experience, and no college name to identify who and where I am. I credit the bulk of my education and wisdom to the Montessori School I attended in kindergarten through 3rd grade and, in addition to the people I grew up with, to the time I have spent volunteering at the teen shelter as a peer advocate. I am thankful to have lived in the city for my whole life and infinitely grateful to this work I have been able to participate in which has made the place I live really become my home. Working with homeless teens has taught me that real homes are not places but are in other people's spirits. I think a lot about my past, try to be present everywhere I go and in the future, and plan to become more of myself.

Rich Exchange

Tonight the cowboy was at the house again. We've become his home since he arrived from the Northwest. I don't think he is any surer than we are how or why he ended up here. Tonight was his 18th birthday, although it seemed like everything around him was dying, not being born. All his plans fell through, and he'd become homeless again.

I took a break to go to the nearby high school for an hour or so, where that same night a bunch of students were sleeping outside in boxes to raise awareness and money for the homeless. In awe of the irony, I returned to the house we have for the homeless, and the cowboy was sitting with everyone else eating birthday cake, hopefully giving him reason to celebrate. He asked to talk to me, because he was wondering if I was taking a philosophy class or something, pointing to what I had written on the card I'd made earlier for him. It read, "Happy birthday cowboy, I celebrate that the northwest winds blew you this way and congratulations on discovering one of the greatest and most difficult lessons: that we cannot have room for deep happiness until we've had that space carved out inside of us with deep pain."

I told him that I didn't learn that in class; those are the truths you can only discover on your own, and I'd learned that lesson on my 18th birthday not too long ago by a different path. He understood and said that it really meant a lot to him. And I told him that I really meant it. Then he went outside and I lost track of time, but at some point he came back carrying an old, ugly, yellow jacket and told me to try it on. I told him it looked a little large, but he told me to try it on anyway. Then I understood that he wanted to give it to me, and suddenly it became the most beautiful gift I'd ever received. I wore it the rest of the night.

Interpretation

As it was being experienced, I think this moment was powerful because it was a mutual exchange–one that had nothing to do with money; we could not prove that it was a mutual exchange, but we both knew, while it was happening, that this was a true exchange. I gave him some words I really meant and spent a lot of time thinking about, and he gave me a jacket he had spent a lot of time wearing. So we each gave something that was part of us.

In reflection, it was a powerful moment for two reasons. Many times a client will open up about his or her situation, and we will respond with a list of resources or ideas we have been taught are helpful in those situations. But the youthworker does not really have to be open in the way the client does. Yet at that moment there were no ideas or resources I felt I could offer him. All I could give him was a little awareness I had picked up in my life. And so I opened myself to share something with him while still keeping the focus of the relationship on him and his situation.

The power of that moment also came from the presence we both had while it was going on. After it ended, it was absolutely over. We had a beginning and an ending, and nothing was left unfinished. It was a complete moment. Nothing else would continue out of it; nothing else would have to be said about it between us.

Most significantly, because we were both present and both gave something real of ourselves for that moment, we were not in the history of child and youth care, we were in the history of the world: He was not a client and I was not a worker; we were just two people in life willing to look up for a moment and smile as we passed.

JOSEPH STANLEY

I have been involved in youthwork for 16-17 years. I got my feet wet as a community volunteer at the runaway shelter where I now work as a program therapist. I do individual and family counseling with youth ages 11-17. I have a master's degree in Educational Psychology from University of Wisconsin-Milwaukee. I have also worked in different areas of the field such as a crisis phone service, group homes, mentoring, research, and intensive in-home services over the years while working in some capacity at the Pathfinders program. This is connected to my choice to pursue a career in youthwork.

I grew up on the streets from age 13 into adulthood. I engaged in and experienced the life of the streets. I did not graduate from high school. Through a few positive and nurturing experiences with adults as a youth, I decided to volunteer my time with youth as an adult and never left. I will continue at the shelter and pursue a doctoral degree.

Moment

I received a call from a youth. It was his 15th birthday. He said, "You need to come and get me, Joseph. I'm at my mother's . . . she's being such a bitch." He explained that he was at his mother's home because she took him to an appointment.

At his mother's home (he's currently in foster placement), I walked into a shouting match and felt overwhelmed by the sharp and quick exchanges. It seemed as if neither he nor his mother were ready at that moment for a positive exchange. I sat back with my feet firmly planted so I wouldn't get blown over by the conflict between them. I practiced deep breathing. I visualized every cell in my body. I visualized them relaxing. I breathed and centered myself.

I told mom that it seemed difficult to deal with the anger, language, and threats. I expressed my empathy with the situation. I told her I understood that she was upset because he wasn't staying in school and that she didn't know what to do. I told the youth that he needed to stop yelling at his mother: It was not okay. We gathered his belongings and exited the home. I thanked the mother as we left.

As we drove away, he said that mom just "flipped him off," and, "See Joseph, I told you she was like that." I said that it was hard to deal with that, and that I would be hurt and angry.

Interpretation

Conflict was chronic. Youth and mother needed to be separated. It was a storm in the home, and it did not seem controllable, but I could provide some calm and then a refuge by removing him. The youth and mother had power struggles that became vengeful and hurtful, and at this point they did not did not seem to be able to coexist. Also, a key in my professional relationship was to empathize with both of them. My history and personal experience point to the fact that, at times, the only intervention that is workable is to stabilize the situation by separation. I can intervene by introducing a calming effect.

Moment

Youth called: "Hello!!!" . . . I told my mother that I got kicked out of summer school–"I'm proud that you did that!!!"–"She's pissed."–"What would happen if you apologized?'–"Nothing." Silence Silence–"I'll try"–"Hold on." Five minutes pass. "She's better I guess."–"I'm proud."–"You took a chance" and also, "I'll see you tomorrow . . . thanks for the call . . . I'm proud"–"Thanks"–"Yeah"–"Bye."

Interpretation

He seemed to need my support to carry out his intent. Just being there and present is enough. There are always positives to recognize. Also, my experience and book knowledge support the concept that a positive nurturing adult increases resiliency in youth who have a problematic childhood.

Moment

I stroll down the street–
My mind races
Numerous thoughts–with no cohesion
It has been a busy day–one crisis after another–the next starting
Before the last finished
Remember to breathe
Slowly I breathe in and out
I picture the tension flowing out of by body
A couple of minutes later–the tension is gone

Still thoughts race through my mind
I'm picking up Bob
Bob has a lot of energy–and seems to have a strong effect on his
teachers
He can be a challenge
I'm tired
Remember to breathe–I think about Bob–he can
Remember to breathe
I picture my center as I breathe–tolling toward the school
I laugh–one of us needs to be there
I pull up to the curb–backpack-coat going in every direction
The car door opens
Joseph-Joseph you're late–I'm going to tell my Mother you left
me
I left you–You told me to pick you up at 3pm
Yeah but I wanted you to pick me up early
Oh–I forgot to turn on my superpower mind reading today
Seatbelt
Seat belt is latched
At the same moment the radio is adjusted
Singing begins even before I hear the song
I slowly pull away–wishing I did have superpowers to deal with
the energy
I laugh–Bob laughs
We slowly talk about school/family/his weekend
He speaks rapidly at times
At times I breathe
We move onto what worked for him today–what didn't
I breathe
We laugh

Interpretation

For some of the youth I work with, being centered does not happen
for them. This can lead to barriers for them functioning in the community. One strategy that seems to work is to center myself and provide a
calm in storm.

QUINN WILDER

I was raised through my teens by a youthworker and my stepfather
and started working in a crisis intervention center at 21. I worked with

teens at a YMCA camp, a shelter, a group home, a residential treatment center, an aggression course, and as a mentor on an in-home treatment team. Today I am a father as well as a mentor, a youthwork educator, and an advocate for the development of the youthwork field. My dream is that youthworkers will become fully valued for the important role they play as accessible, skilled, and caring adults in youth's lives.

Singing with Dave and the Girls

>Dave started singing in the big, cold rec-room with the broken TV, shades from the 1970s, and brown institutional furniture.
>
>"Aw, this song is corny," said one of the girls who lived in the group home. "I'm not singing this shit!"
>
>"Then why are you here?" another girl asked.
>
>"To listen to you all," she laughed.
>
>"Let's try again," Dave said, and we both started playing the guitar to an old Beatles tune. I sang it loudly with Dave, and the five girls all sang along. We did the song a few more times. Each time their voices got stronger and the giggles lessened.
>
>"Here's another one," said Dave.
>
>"Oooh, let me see this one, how does it go?"

Interpretation

I was a brand new youthworker in a residential program for girls. I had not developed much of a rapport with any of the girls and, although I liked Dave, I was not sure about his ability to connect with them either. The girls seemed frequently angry and defiant about everything that happened on the unit, so when Dave suggested having a singing group, I did not see it happening. I really did not want to do it, although deep inside I believed that it was a good thing to do. Ideally, we should be able to get together and sing. So with Dave's help, I made myself do it. I thought the girls would just stare at Dave and me, laugh, and walk away.

What made this an important moment for everyone was that in the context of anger, fighting, and anxiety, youth and youthworkers were able to have fun together. I had to face my fears about singing to an unknown, possibly hostile crowd. The experience became an opportunity to break through the hostility and just be persons singing together. It also helped me find ways to connect with them in a more personal, human way than I experienced with most other adults.

Meeting the Mentor

I drive up the driveway to the house. It's August, a hot sunny day. I step out of the car, see a 12-year-old boy standing 20 yards away in his backyard and looking at me out of the corner of his eye. I walk towards him. "Hi Max. I'm Quinn, your mentor." I extend my hand. He hesitates, expressionless, and says, "Hi," shaking my hand weakly. "You wanna' show me around the neighborhood?"

"Sure," he says. We walk down the driveway. "That's the Benson's house over there. Ted, he's kind of dorky, but he's got a real cool bike. Do you like the Smashing Pumpkins?"

Interpretation

I had done youthwork in several capacities and was starting graduate school. I needed a part-time job and wanted to be able to work intensively with teenagers. I was told about a mentoring program that placed mentors on a treatment team. The mentors were supposed to provide relief for parents under stress. I had been briefed on the family to which I had been assigned. Their 12-year-old had Tourette's Syndrome and had recently been discovered on the roof of his home threatening to jump.

Over time our relationship became very important to Max and the family. I think the fact that we were able to talk freely and feel comfortable with each other quickly in a rather novel situation anticipated our success. Also, I think Max realized that he was at risk of being separated from his family and that I represented a great opportunity to keep that from happening.

The literature on youthwork interactions refers to rhythm, movement, and presence as being central to connecting with youth. These themes are evident in my story. There is little required of the mentee at first, then gradually he is given an opportunity to communicate more freely and with greater personal commitment. This is reflected at the end of the story when the mentee initiates a topic of interest to him–music–and shows curiosity about my own interests, searching for a connection.

AMY EVANS

I grew up in a town of 10,000 people in a middle-class family, and I am grateful for the safety, nurture, and privileges of my childhood. I now live in a diverse city of 650,000 people that has allowed me to expand my comfort level, insights, philosophy, knowledge, gratitude, and enjoyment.

I obtained a Master of Social Work degree in 1998. I have volunteered with women, children, and answering crisis lines. I did my internships in a teen crisis shelter and in an acute psychiatric unit for children. I was employed with the teen crisis shelter for five years and then went for one year to do intensive in-home family therapy. Presently I am working with an exciting program for children who have been sexually abused doing individual, group, and in-home family therapy.

I am challenged to learn many things in many different ways through clients, co-workers, trainings, friends, etc. I am also able to challenge others' ways of thinking or doing things in order for my experiences to prosper positive changes for new insights, programs, all of which I appreciate, thrive on, and grow from.

Moment

I stepped out of my car and began walking the path to the front of the school in hopes of having a session with a 10-year-old girl, Katie. I was feeling relaxed and thinking about possible ideas to address in the session and a possible art work project to incorporate if Katie was in a stable, relaxed mood with no crisis on her mind. Over the past several months Katie had experienced several sexual abuse crises.

I asked the office staff to call Katie down for a private session in the conference room. Approximately 5 minutes later, Katie arrived, at which time I began to feel some anxiety about which big issue she would raise.

Upon seeing me, Katie smiled shyly, shrugged her body, continued toward me, and reached out for a hug. We hugged for a brief moment and walked toward our meeting room.

After getting seated close to each other at the table, I asked Katie how she was doing, and she said she did not know. We engaged in some small talk about her day in school and some interactions with her foster family that occurred the night before. There was then an obvious pause of silence in which we both engaged in deep-eye contact. Then I asked her what she was thinking about.

Katie slowly began telling me her thoughts about the sexual abuse she had endured over the years by several perpetrators. I asked her if she wanted to draw some pictures of the most frequent thoughts she was having. "Yes," she said and drew a picture of two different perpetrators abusing her.

She felt that it was her fault she was in foster care, and she feared her stepmother would go to jail. We talked about these abuse experiences, her fear and confusion, and the social service policy origins and causes of events for which she understand-ably–but mistakenly–felt responsible. I conveyed to her again that telling about the abuse was brave and how important it is to take care of herself. We discussed possible consequences for a particu-lar perpetrator and how this might help the stepmother get help. Katie nodded her head, affirming some of the ideas we discussed.

Katie then said, "I hope . . . [the perpetrator] doesn't go to jail," and she sobbed as she rested her head on the table, the side of her face against the table and her chin trembling as she cried.

I allowed her to cry a bit without saying anything as I thought about how overwhelmed, confused, and alone she must have felt.

After some time passed I told Katie I was glad she was let-ting out some of her feelings. Katie lifted her head and wiped her face.

I briefly summarized the events occurring in her life, the things that she was doing well, and the good things that were happening to her.

We talked about what she could do between now and the next session. Katie seemed relaxed, sad, and somewhat tired. We talked a minute with the office staff on our way out. In the hallway I told Katie to take it easy and that I would see her next week. She said, "Okay," and gave me a longer hug than she did earlier. Then she said, "Bye," turned around, and walked down the hallway.

I walked out of the school thinking about what had just oc-curred and feeling sad, powerless, and grateful for being part of Katie's life.

Interpretation

With reflection, I see the significance of this moment is that Katie had one solid person in her life with whom to talk with about her feel-ings and thoughts. The outcomes/answers for Katie's questions were unknown in terms of taking action or making changes; just being to-gether was the best thing that could happen. This was something valu-able and all that was available: to simply validate that someone's life is difficult.

It was a break in Katie's school day, a chance to open up and let out some of her stressful thoughts and feelings to a person with whom she felt comfortable.

A theme that I have learned from a valued co-worker and others is that to "show up" with youth (to be available and open to where the youth is at without a rigid agenda of what to discuss or do) is sometimes the most valuable thing one can do. This also takes the pressure off me to "fix" things and allows me to be there for the youth. It is a freeing, powerful idea. It allows youth to be where they are at and gives me an opportunity to process growth from that point.

Jenny

I pick up 9-year-old Jenny for a session and bring her back to the agency to meet in an office. We pull into the parking lot, and Jenny cannot open her door as it is an old car and the door sticks. I tell her I will be right around to open it. I close my door and go around and open her door. Jenny steps out and looks at me, smiles with a gleam in her eye, and says, "Ready, set, go." We race to the door as we do before and after most sessions. When we're almost at the entrance, Jenny lets me win.

As we walk up the stairs and toward the office I try to stay in step with Jenny, but she continues to slow down and walk behind me rather than with me. I am nervous and tense, a bit out of control and concerned about what she might do to defy or rebel against me and about being embarrassed in front of some co-workers.

We arrive at my co-worker's private, available office space. I do not have a private office space of my own. I unlock the door and Jenny walks in first. I follow and close the door. While I set up some of the materials we will use in the session, Jenny looks at the things in the office, touching some of them, and asking questions about others. After a minute I sit in a chair across from her. I ask if she wants to sit on the floor as I move to the floor. "Okay," she says, and moves to the floor.

I tell her that today we will finish the activity we started last week, and I unroll the big drawing of a girl on a piece of paper she made last week. I describe the plan for the activity and ask her to define some words about different forms of sexual abuse.

"I don't know," she says about all of them. As I explain Jenny hides her face in her hands and turns her body a bit to the side away from me. I then say, "Okay, now we can begin the activity." I bring out stickers for her to put on the drawing in various places where the girl in the drawing was abused. Jenny grabs a sticker and places it on the body. This continues for awhile, and each time I ask her to identify that form of abuse. After a few times Jenny throws the sticker and says she does not want to do this. I ask her if I can take a turn and she says, "Yes."

As I take a sticker she grabs it from me and does it herself. A few moments later this happens again, and I take a sticker and place it on the picture. Jenny tries to remove the sticker, and I cover it with my hand: "No–leave it there."

"That is gross." Again I tell her that the body part is not gross. It is just a body part; the abuse is what is bad. I repeat this two more times. Jenny then takes more stickers and places them on the body even at those places she earlier thought were "gross." At one point, Jenny takes the candy I gave her earlier, unwraps it, and throws it. I ask her if she wants to eat it or throw it away. "Eat it." I tell her to pick it up to eat or throw it away. Jenny picks it up in her hand, placing a piece in her mouth.

We then place band aids over each sticker and identify a person she could tell if this type of abuse occurs.

"I don't want to do it."

I say, "We can either do this or I can take you home now."

"Okay I'll do it," and she grabs a band aid. Jenny completes the activity and suggests several people who she can tell, and she suggests a therapist for certain types as well, which I feel is a small amount of trust between us, even if she is very guarded.

"You did a great job today knowing a lot about different types of abuse and knowing who you can talk to about abuse."

We both put on our coats and exit the office. Jenny walks far ahead of me and does not wait to race to the car. I walk directly toward the car, and she walks a longer way around to get to the car. I feel worried about her feelings. I feel anxious and I'm trying to stay calm, relaxing my body, and focusing on my breathing so she hopefully will not see that I'm bothered by this feeling of disconnection/rebellion from her. We drive to her home in silence. I ask her if she wants to race, and she keeps walking to her front door. Her guardian is near the door, and says she and the kids are going to visit their mom now. Jenny jumps up and down, smiles, and runs upstairs. I confirm my return date and tell the guardian that Jenny did a good job. As I leave, I say "See you later" to the aunt, and Jenny pokes her head around the upstairs area. "Bye Amy."

"See you later Jenny."

Interpretation

I believe Jenny feels alone in her world and as though she cannot trust or relate to anyone. When I placed some stickers on the body and would not allow them to be removed, I set a boundary for her as well as gave her permission to acknowledge abuse as fact and something outside of herself. Until age 8, Jenny lived with unpredictability in fearful, dangerous, powerless situations.

Jenny may not have consciously and confidently understood that she can trust a therapist to talk about difficult times, but did acknowledge that it is a possibility.

Jenny seems to be in control of the amount of intimacy that she will allow to occur, specifically, letting me win in the race, walking with me and not walking with me, disclosing and/or not disclosing parts of herself or her life.

Jenny needs to have some control or needs to know what she does have control over, and she does things consciously or unconsciously that provides me with the responsibility of providing her necessary boundaries, something she probably did not have a lot of safe direction about in her earlier childhood years.

Jenny also desires a relationship with her mom, which has not always been possible. When Jenny found out she was going to visit her mom, she felt excited and possibly secure for that one moment and was able to let go of her guard and reach out for a friendly goodbye. A dependable, positive relationship with her mom seems to be a lot of what she needs and desires.

Journey

I'm on my way to a home visit to see two children and their mother, if they are all at home as planned; otherwise I will meet with whoever is there when I arrive. I am feeling confident but nervous, because this family is volatile, and a couple days ago the mom contacted my supervisor frustrated and angry that her kids are worse since being in counseling, and she cannot take any more of their disrespectful attitudes and may pull them out of therapy.

I am driving down the freeway on the way. I notice other cars and trucks passing me by. I am going the speed limit. The sun is out with rather soft light. Traffic is steady and peaceful, although I am not noticing too much of what is around me, as I am absorbing the peace and wishing it could last longer before having to exit the freeway. As I am driving I am aware that she may yell at the children or at me during the session. I am centering myself, reminding myself this is not about me, and staying open to whatever may seem the best in facilitating this family's relationships with each other and other issues. I am taking deep breaths and trying to calm myself, although I am unable to completely do so. I am also reminding myself that I have a good connection with each of the children and a fairly good connection with the mom, so no matter what happens today in the session it seems like it will work itself out in the end, or the worst case scenario would be that the therapy relationship will end. Life goes on and the next client will be assigned to me.

As I pull into their parking lot I don't look up to the third floor window so that I avoid a possible angry glance from mom. I walk into the apartment complex and say a prayer to ask for the strength to do with this family whatever I am supposed to do today, including accepting that nothing can be done today, and thinking at the same time that that would still be something.

I walk up to the third floor, turn right down the hall, and knock at the door.

Interpretation

I am about to voluntarily encounter a potentially tense situation. It is currently my job, and I am getting paid for it and, spiritually, it feels like my journey at this time, but sometimes I would like to avoid it. This is how I often feel prior to arriving at many sessions with individuals and families, because what will be encountered is unpredictable.

The interpretation of the following stories is left up to the reader.

MARK KRUEGER

Grilled Cheese

I savor the aroma. Alan looks at the tray of sandwiches. He's hungry after a morning of kickball, and grilled cheese is his favorite lunch. It's mine too.

"Take a damn sandwich!" demands Bill, a stocky 15-year-old.

"Relax, Bill," I say and turn my back to take a tray of tomato soup from Wilda, the kitchen helper. Meanwhile, Alan loads his plate and passes the sandwiches.

"Alan took five sandwiches, Alan took five sandwiches," says Tony in a sing-song voice.

Alan slugs Tony in the arm just as I turn around. "Alan, put three back and take that cap off."

Alan smiles and puts three back, making sure to leave a thumb print in each one.

"God, I'm not going to eat those; I'll get AIDS," says Rick, who is sitting across the table.

Alan pushes his chair back and cocks his fist.

"Knock it off, Alan! That was ridiculous. There's enough for everyone. Now pull your chair up!" I say.

Alan inches his chair forward. "No there isn't. This is all I'll probably get, just like last time."

"Bull, you had about ten," Bill says.

"Shut up porker," Alan says and puffs his cheeks.

"Alan–Bill, stop it now!" I say.

"I'm not eating this tomato soup. It looks like blood," Tully, another boy, says.

"Just try a few spoonfuls . . ." as a chair slides, with anger, across the floor, propelled by another boy. His youthworker, Debbie, has him pick up the chair and walks him into the hall.

"You workers never do what you say you're going to do," Alan says.

"What do you mean?" I ask, frustrated by what's transpired.

"You said you'd get me a foster home, but you never do."

"Yeah," says Rick.

"Your social worker has been looking, but you're not acting today like you're ready."

"I've been ready for 3 months and you know it."

Bill chuckles.

Alan stands, chest out, and whips a sandwich at Bill.

Tully displays a mouthful of mush.

The Stranger

Bobby, a 13-year-old with some cognitive limitations, runs up to me. "It's 4:00, can I go off grounds?"

"Yes, you've earned the right to go off now by yourself. But you have to be back by 4:45 to get ready for dinner."

"I'm just going down the street to the variety store to get some Life Savers. Get some money from my bank."

I stare at him.

"Please."

I smile and we walk down the hall to the office where we keep the boys' banks. I give him fifty cents. "How much change will you get?"

He uses his fingers to count. "Ten cents."

"Good, now don't forget. 4:45."

"I won't."

He runs down the stairs and skips along the street as I watch from the second floor where I'm playing pool with the other boys. This is his first trip alone into the community since he first came, and he seems ecstatic.

He returns at 4:40 with a big smile on his face. I greet him at the door. "How'd it go?"

"Great." He holds out one hand to show me the Life Savers, and then gives me the ten cents for his bank.

"You even got back early," I say, delighted.

"Yeah, you know what, Mark?"

"No, what?"

"I got a ride back."

"From who?" my expression changes.

"An old man sitting on a bench outside the variety store."

"Bobby, your first time into the community and now we have to restrict you," I say, showing my disappointment.

"Why?" he says, seemingly very surprised.

"How many times have we told you not to take a ride from a stranger?"

Angry and upset, he clenches his fist, turns and begins to walk back to his room. Then he stops, faces me and says, "How the fuck was I supposed to know he was a stranger?!"

QUINN WILDER

Three Moments

"Hey, what's that?"

A boy points at the drumsticks I'm holding in my hands.

"Drumsticks," I say. "Wanna' learn how to play?"

"Right now?" His eyes light up with excitement.

"Yeah, we're going upstairs to play, wanna' come?" He eagerly nods.

He and several others follow me in a line as I walk towards the back of the huge recreation room. I'm heading toward some doors, but I have no idea how to get upstairs. I step sideways to get next to the youth behind me and ask him if we can get upstairs by going this way. He nods his head. I'm not sure if he understood me. We open a door to enter the small room, and there's a group of young girls playing a boom box and learning a dance routine. We exit and some of the youths who were following me start asking how to get upstairs. One older boy tells me it's "over here," towards the front of the building, and we head that direction. By now, our group has doubled in size, and we go upstairs where the executive director is unlocking the door.

"You're locked in with them now," he says to me with a smile, and he heads back downstairs.

We walk through a large, empty room, out a caged door, and into another room with a desk and a linoleum table. I show them some drumming beats and techniques, give them each a pair of sticks, and we play on that table for about 25 minutes. I say goodbye and some of them ask me if I'm going to come back for more drumming. I tell them I might be able to come back sometime, but that it depends on whether my drum program at another youth center works out. I wave to the executive director across the room, the drummers filter back into other activities, and I head out the door.

Untitled

We pull into the parking lot of the park and, as soon as the car stops, two of the boys jump out and head for the river.

"Where are you guys going?" I ask.

"My uncle took me here once to fish," one of the boys shouts to me across the parking lot. The youngest brother and I head in their direction. I arrive to find the brothers standing on a trail by the river, watching people fish. Their eyes are lit up with excitement, and I think to myself that if I get to see them again, I will try to take them fishing.

"Do you want to play the game I was talking about?"

"Yeah," the oldest replies.

"Let's go find a good place," I say, and we quickly walk together across the parking lot, talking about fishing. We cross the park road together and arrive at a small clearing between several trees. It's a bright, sunny, hot day.

"This place looks good; let's just play catch for awhile," I say, and I toss the Frisbee to the oldest brother. He jumps up into the air, catches it, lands on his feet, and looks at it with a surprised expression on his face. Then he throws it to one of his brothers. We play catch, me leading them so they have to run to catch it.

"Ready to play ultimate Frisbee?" I ask.

"Yeah," the youngest responds.

"You can't run while holding the Frisbee and to score a point you have to throw it so it hits this tree."

The boys start out hesitantly, forgetting not to run with the Frisbee but figuring out their strategies and very quickly they are scoring points, diving for the Frisbee, and jumping up and down screaming and laughing at each other.

"Wanna take a break?"

We drop simultaneously to the ground, smiles on our faces, exhausted, lying on the grass, and catching our breath.

"Ya' like it?" I ask them. They nod their heads enthusiastically.

Untitled

The strong, musty smell that is always here fills the large recreation room in the unit. Taking up space is an old TV, a coffee table, some plastic chairs, and the usual "special" brown furniture made to withstand use by "at-risk" youth. The girls are sitting around a short, round table with me in a plastic chair as I lead a group.

"I'm leaving the unit, quitting the job for grad school, and this is my second-to-last day," I say.

"What do we have to do this stupid group for?"

"What do you have in those bags?"

"These are surprises. I'm going to take them out. Let me say something first, though, once everyone is sitting down and can hear me. Okay, you know already that tomorrow is my last day here. I am going back to school so I can become a social worker. Someday, you too might be saying goodbye to people you care about so you can go to school or take on a new challenge in your life."

"Yeah, so what's in the bags?"

"I have something I want to give each of you before I leave."

I move around the circle of girls, taking an item out of the bag, describing its significance, and giving it to the girl.

"And Vikki, we've been through a lot together here, and you're going to get a new primary worker. So I wanted to leave you with something to help you get by. We all know how you can get loud and angry and how that's gotten you in trouble, and you've gotten better at keeping yourself calm and speaking more softly in order to get treated with respect. I want you to do well after I'm gone, so I made you this."

I take out a large cone made out of construction paper, with writing on it.

"This is the Vikki Voice Controller, and when you start getting mad and you have to scream and yell at someone, just put the big end on your mouth, and it comes out quiet on the other end."

I smile, the other girls laugh, and Vikki smiles and laughs as I hand it to her.

JOHN KORSMO

Red Cliff Trip (Self-Talk)

Why did I agree to do this?
Why didn't I take it more seriously and do it the right way?
Why didn't I have the guys get together a few times to meet each other and at the very least cut some of the tension?
Wonder what they are thinking, heading up to the middle of nowhere with some guy they never met?
What an idiot.
Bad small talk. Bad air. Bad idea.
Its loud; I am not in any sort of control.
I am the driver–that's it.
I screwed up with this group. I should have spent time getting to know them.
I didn't have time.
I agreed to fill-in at the last minute.
It's not my fault.
Make something good happen.
Don't let them gun so hard on each other.
I can see the two to watch out for.
I need an ally.
Which one?

RICK FLOWERS

Personal Sketch

I wandered into youthwork as a young, hard-charging Marine in the early 1990s. I was stationed at an American Embassy overseas where there were not many American youth. I was in my early twenties and was viewed as both youthful and mature. That's the image that the Marines had. The American youth gravitated naturally toward us due to our uniqueness compared to the rest of the diplomatic community. We were a novelty. As a result we started planning activities for youth. It started with scavenger hunts and eventually led to starting a Scout troop and soccer team that competed against the local youth. I have been involved with youth in some capacity ever since then. Today I do mentoring and assist in managing a teen night and variety club.

Big Ray: Moment from My Youth

There was nothing unusual about the day. We were on our way to the back alley to shoot some hoops. Ken and I were dribbling the ball down the alley and making fancy passes to each other and talking about what we were going to do on the court, a large, white, barn-shaped garage with the basketball hoop. We always wondered what was in it, since we never saw a car enter or leave the garage.

We finally arrive at the court and Ken says immediately, "Let's play some H-O-R-S-E." I agree and let Ken take the first shot. He makes a lay-up and I reply, "That ain't shit," and proceed to make a lay-up. Just as Ken starts to try another shot, two people suddenly appear at the court. It's big Ray and someone else. Then another person shows up. We scrap the H-O-R-S-E game and start a game of Hustle.

"What you got Ken, you can't fuck with this."

"I'm 'a take your ass to the hole this time."

The ball is in Ken's hand now, and I'm telling him, "You ain't shit, your ass too scared to shoot it from there." Ken misses the shot.

Big Ray has the ball now. He holds the ball, looks at me, and says, "What would your mamma say if she heard you out here cussing like that?" Big Ray was only a couple of years older than me, but he appeared to be much older and was viewed at as one of the older guys.

My first thought was to tell him that she wouldn't say "shit," but the words would not come out, perhaps from fear that he might go and ask my mom. My second thought was to say, "Fuck you"; that didn't happen either. Instead I was frozen with what seemed to be an audience waiting for a response. I finally managed to say, "I don't know," but I did know. I knew that I would stop cursing from then on.

ARCELIA (CHITA) MARTINEZ

Easy flowing, happy-as-can-be, no trouble in the world; that was what I experienced as a child. Lost, confused, scared, a slap in the face is what I experienced as I grew older. My parents did what they could. I do not blame them. They only taught us what they knew. With their support, now I'm "Una Latina Fina!"

While remembering how tough it was, I can only imagine what our youth go through now. I stop and think time and time again, "Where would I be without the support of my family and youthworkers who helped me with my struggles?" Youth today do not have the support at home. How tough is that? It's very tough! I see it! I will assist the youth to see outside the box. Just the same as how I had to learn. That's why my heart is with the youth! *I am an Agent of Growth and Development.*

A Moment in Time Connecting with Youth

I met this young lady who was assigned to me through the First Time Juvenile Offender Program. My supervisor at the time asked me if I could mentor her, because other mentors were having a hard time helping her complete the program. So my supervisor felt that I was a good match for her, since we had similar backgrounds. I set up an appointment to meet with her.

Mimi looked at me with a straight face. I looked at her with the same look and then smiled. "What's up, girly?"

"What up?" she responded.

"Are you Mimi?"

"Yeah, I'm Mimi." She looked the other way.

"I'm Chita!"

She looked at me with a cracked smile. "So we finally meet, huh?"

"Yeah I had to come." I put my hand on Mimi's shoulder and guided her outside. We sat on the ledge of the sidewalk under the pleasant warm sun. "So, Mimi why are you in this program?"

"I got into a fight at school."

"Mmmm, so you got caught up, huh?"

"Well ol' girl looked at me crazy and was trying to talk smack!" She continued to tell me what happened.

"What happened to the other girl?"

"Nothing really. I got more in trouble than she did and she is the one who started it!"

"Yeah, Mimi, but you got physical."

"Well, yeah, she got me so pissed-off!"

"So you decided to swing."

She got quiet. The sun was beaming; she was sweating and getting irritated, and she was moving around. I said, "Yeah, I probably would have hit her if it was me, but that was back in the day when that is all I knew to do."

She looked at me with a surprising look, "What do you mean?"

"Well, before I didn't know how to speak on things in those situations."

"What do you say now?"

"I would question her and ask her why are you giving me so much attention?"

"What would their response be?"

"Well, they would get caught off guard and wouldn't say anything because they don't expect that!"

"I never thought of that, I get too angry too quick."

"Well try it and see what happens—it sure does beat getting a ticket and having to be in this program!"

PAMELA RAMSEY[1]

My most memorable early childhood moments (until age 9) are of Greenwood, Mississippi. Life seemed so "FREE." I was able to roam the streets ("out backwoods") with my siblings and friends. We really experienced life and became one with nature. It saddens me to see that youth today are not afforded those types of opportunities, not even in

Greenwood. We moved to Milwaukee when I was 9 years old and, boy, did life change for us. This was a very big city compared to Greenwood, and I got lost in it many times and in many ways (mentally and physically). By the age of 17 I became a mother. That was truly life changing–some good, some bad, some beautiful, and some ugly. Without explaining, let me just say that my daughter is now 18 years old and "it's all good!" My childhood and parenting are what gave me the desire to help others, particularly youth.

I became involved in the child and youth care field after seeing the devastation that life was placing on their innocent lives by way of poverty, drugs, racism, etc. My passion at that time was to work with prenatal substance-exposed children. I soon became a foster parent to one of my nephews while pursuing my BA in Social Work. I officially began working in the child and youth care field in May 1994, and have done so since, although my role has changed. I have now obtained my MA in School and Community Counseling. My interests are still with youth and families and will always be.

Independent Living

I went to K-Mart on South 27th Street to find some sheer curtains I had been looking for. I was hopeful, yet anxious to get out of the store, because it was very crowded and messy, as it was near Christmas. As I strolled down the aisle, I noticed a young lady across the way who looked very familiar. I couldn't see her face very well and found myself staring. As we moved closer, I realized I knew her.

Her story flashed through my mind: the middle child of three sisters–no children–struggled with school but managed to finish. Worked at Burger King off Chase, and a great money saver. She must be 22-23 now. "What is she doing now? What's her name? What is her name? She's getting closer–What is her name?" I hate it when I don't remember their names. "What will I say to her? Will she remember me?"

She's here. "Well-well, look who we have here! How are you doing?"

"Hi." She doesn't remember me, but it was obvious from the frown on her forehead that I looked familiar to her based on the frown in her forehead. She screamed: "Oh, I remember you, but I am sorry that I don't remember your name."

"Pam. I don't remember your name either."

"Natash. What school did you go to?"

I had to blush after that–was she pulling my leg with that line? "I am Pam Ramsey from the Independent Living Program."

"Oh-yeah!" You look so different with your hair like that . . . you used to wear braids–right?"

"Yeah I did. So how have you been?"

"Fine. I am working at TCF Bank. I had a baby six months ago and I am engaged to get married in July."

"Wow, that's great!" I said. "You look very happy."

"I am. You remember my sister, Denise, the oldest?"

I nodded.

"She had a baby too–a girl. I had a boy. She is married and they bought a house. She works for the city."

"You girls have really grown up," I said.

"Do you remember my baby sister, Jonah? She got two babies and is pregnant again. She's still messing up. We try to talk to her, but she ain't trying to hear us."

"Keep talking; she'll hear you one day. Don't give up on her. She'll find her way in her own time."

"I know–she'll do good for awhile and then mess up, so I know she can when she want to. Are you still doing those groups?"

"I am still with ILP, but I stopped doing groups. I plan to start back in January though."

"That was a good program, it helped me a lot. Cause I didn't know what I was going to do. I remember when Denise used to come home talking about it, I couldn't wait to turn 16 to join. I really liked it."

"Alright, now you're making me blush," I said.

"I'm for real though."

"Well, thank you. How old is Jonah?"

"Nineteen."

"Well, here, take my card and have her give me a call."

"Do you think you can help her?"

"Honey, nothing beats a failure but a try."

"I hope so–she needs all the help she can get."

"I'm not going to hold you up, plus I have to get going. You *all* should call me sometime and tell Jonah, Denise and your aunt I said hello."

She leaned towards me and gave me the warmest hug. We looked at each other, smiled and said good-bye.

NOTE

1. For a few months, Pamela Ramsey brought a wonderful sense of wisdom and insight to our group. At the time she was the program director and outreach worker for an independent living program. She has now moved on to another job.

Chapter Four
Three Sketches

Recently I have been experimenting with juxtaposing events from
my life before and after my years as a youthworker with my experience
as a youthworker in fictitious narratives that ring true with my experiences. My goal is to explore how these experiences are intertwined. A
few members of our research group have also been conducting their
own inquiries. Following are three works in progress or sketches. The
first represents my formative years, or the experience that seemed to
shape me as a youth and adult. The second is an early event with a
youth, and the third an event with the same youth much later.

PAVILION (1957)

"How did you feel when our father died?" my uncle asks my father.
"Like the boy in James Joyce's story about the dead priest: sad and
relieved, I guess."
"It was different when mother died, wasn't it," my uncle says.
"Yes, God forgive us if we ever lose the benignity she tried to instill
in us."
"Yes, God forgive them," my mother says to my aunt. They're in the
kitchen of our second story flat on Milwaukee's Northwest side. My
older brother is asleep in the bed next to mine. I'm 14 going on 15. It's
late summer, 1957.
After the company is gone, I get dressed. The house is dark. Something
moves. My father is dancing in the living room in the shadows of the elm

[Haworth co-indexing entry note]: "Three Sketches." Krueger, Mark. Co-published simultaneously in
Child & Youth Services (The Haworth Press, Inc.) Vol. 26, No. 1, 2004, pp. 77-89; and: *Themes and Stories in
Youthwork Practice* (ed: Mark Krueger) The Haworth Press, Inc., 2004, pp. 77-89. Single or multiple copies
of this article are available for a fee from The Haworth Document Delivery Service [1-800-HAWORTH, 9:00
a.m. - 5:00 p.m. (EST). E-mail address: docdelivery@haworthpress.com].

trees that cathedral the narrow street in front of the house. Hidden out of sight, I watch. He's still wearing the shirt and tie he wore to the life insurance company where he has worked all his adult life. His hands are in his pockets, and his pants legs are raised. He is smiling, but his eyes seem far away.

1996

An old woman puts out her cigarette and enters the church with "The Glory of God and His Most Blessed Mother" carved in stone above the doorway. After mass, she comes across the street to the coffee shop. I'm writing in the sunlight of a window seat. Her face is painted like a small girl. It's 1996.

"Hello," says the owner, a conversationalist, who is behind the counter.

"Hi." She sits down on a stool and puts her cigarette on the lip of the glass ashtray. "My girlfriend is coming this weekend."

"How nice."

"We were in the same club in high school. We're going to the beach."

The owner nods and fills another customer's cup.

She reaches for the cigarette; to herself: "I got a new swim suit. Maybe we'll take my beach umbrella too."

"That's good," a young woman seated down the counter from her says with a smile.

"Oh, you probably got a two-piece."

1957

I grab the car keys from the kitchen table, tiptoe down the back stairs, step outside, take a deep breath of the night air, and back the Dodge out of the garage and close the doors. Rows of clapboard duplexes and back porches line the alley, the houses and people in them familiar from walking to the grocery store and in games of kick-the-can.

At the end of the alley, I turn east. The street is bathed in the warm glow of streetlights. A pigeon disappears beneath the hood and reappears in the windshield eyeball-to-eyeball with me. The schoolyard where I play basketball and the cemetery where my brother taught me to drive pass on the left. When I reach Lake Michigan, I park next to the pavilion, which sits on the bluffs like a balcony above nature's great symphony, and dream of being at sea.

1917

From the step of a car, the passengers' silhouettes are hidden momentarily behind the passing girders. My grandfather rides the train to the yard, then takes the trolley to his bungalow on the south side of Milwaukee on the corner of Bow and Arrow streets. My grandmother greets him at the door. He looks handsome in his conductor's uniform. She sits across from him at the dining room table. Their sons, Will (my father) and Charles, were fed earlier and put to bed. WWI just ended.

"The roof is leaking," she says.

"I'll take a look at it tomorrow."

After dinner he goes to Turner Hall. The Turners are a society of German free thinkers, pacifists, and gymnasts. He drinks a few beers and talks with his friends about his travels. When he gets home, he read Nietzsche: "All philosophers have the failing of thinking man is now," and falls asleep with a book in his lap.

In the morning, he climbs on the roof to fix the leak. He works at a steady pace. Ships in the harbor and cream brick buildings downtown are visible. As the sun slowly sinks beneath the elms, he feels a slight chill.

1957

I repeat the word pavilion over and over again until the sound of the word seems strange and meaningless.

> "... a site of linguistic self-consciousness and a point on the map of the modern world that may only be a projection of our desire to give our knowledge a shape that is foreign to or other than it. Above all it is a place that is named." I read Seamus Dean's explanation of Joyce's use of language to name place in the "Introduction to the Penguin Books" 1993 edition of A Portrait of the Artist as a Young Man.

1957

The next day after school, Russo and I take the North Shore electric train to the jazz festival in Chicago. He has a brush haircut; I have a duck's tail. We're both wearing leather jackets. The landscape is a blur, an endless stream of farms and telephone poles.

"I'm thinking of getting my ear pierced like you," I say to my son on the Charles Bridge in Prague shortly after the Velvet Revolution.

"You'll just look like a middle-aged guy trying to be cool." He smiles and hands an earring back to a young woman sitting on a blanket.

We leave the Charles Bridge and walk past Kafka's father's store to a pub in Old Town where we're seated with two young Hungarian men. Devon speaks to them in French. One is a carpenter; the other a tailor.

"They know where I can get a Soviet Army coat," Devon says.

"Go ahead, I'll meet you later on the bridge."

He leaves. I stay and have a sandwich and then return to the bridge after walking slowly through Old Town. The night sky is clear, the water calm. I look at the castle where Vaclav Havel, who wrote for the Theatre of the Absurd and is now the president, lives. Behind me an old man is playing the accordion, his arms opening and closing the billows.

"What are you thinking?" Devon asks. He's wearing the long Soviet coat. The light is at his back, his silhouette tall, faceless, and his voice smooth, like the water that flows under the bridge.

"Nothing."

Slowly the farmland gives way to brown-brick buildings and then taller and taller buildings. From the train station, we walk inland. The city is like another planet: canyons of skyscrapers that block the sun, drunks, students, and businessmen all mixed together. We arrive at Chicago Stadium early and toss coins with two other boys. Men in cardigan sweaters and women in evening gowns begin to arrive. Between us, we win a buck. The stadium is almost full. We mill around, find our seats, and wait. Eventually the buzz of the crowd gives way to the mellow sound of Coleman Hawkin's saxophone followed by J. J. Johnson, Dave Brubeck, Ella Fitzgerald (sweet Ella) and Miles Davis, with his back to the crowd. At first the music comes at me in a cacophony of bits and pieces the way my life does, but then it is as if I'm floating above the crowd.

1968

"See the cardinal?," Suzanne says a few days after I meet her, as we walk along the bluffs in the park above the lake in the late 1960s.

"No, I'm partially color blind."

She smiles, puts her hands on my head, and gently turns it toward a branch in a tree. "See there?"

"Yes," I pretend.

We sit under a tree. "Do you ever think there are no words for feelings?" I ask.

"Yes. That's why I paint."

"But images, like words, are symbols. Do you mix images until all feeling is lost?"

"I don't think much when I paint."

"When did you know you wanted to be an artist?"

"It's all I ever wanted to be."

That evening she gives me a drawing of a naked man crouched in a beam of light. He's bald with long, lean muscles and sunken eyes and does not cast a shadow in the light at his feet. I hang it at the head of my bed. In the morning, her gentle breaths fall in steady beats on my chest.

1957

High from the music, we walk toward the lake. People walk in and out of nightclubs. A picture of a woman on a swing with tassels on her breasts is framed in the cutout of a star.

"You boys ain't 15, much less 21," the doorman says.

I pull Russo by the arm. On Michigan Avenue he proclaims the Prudential Building the tallest in the world. We walk across Grant Park. A man is fishing. He has broken teeth and a torn jacket.

"Catch anything?" Russo asks.

"No, not yet," the man says.

"What you using?" I ask.

"Bacon."

"Bull," Russo says.

The man reaches in his jacket, pulls out a package wrapped in wax paper, unfolds the paper, and shows us the bacon. The high begins to wear off. I turn my back to the lake like Miles Davis.

1972

Beads separate the bedroom from the living room in our small, attic apartment. She works on the floor, crouched over a canvas like a butterfly perched on a daisy, paint on her hands and face, the mandalas and serpents an extension of the movement of her arm. Late at night, I sit with my back to the bookcase, her work just beyond my reach, Fire and Rain, Sweet Baby Jane on the reel-to-reel tape player.

In summer, Devon pretzels out between her legs with double joints and a slight case of jaundice, looking just like the painting she did beforehand: the moonchild with cream eyelids and lashes of fine sable hair. While she breastfeeds him, I walk out on the breakwater that separates the lake from the harbor.

1957

"Never heard of that before," I say.

The man looks at me. "Probably a lot of things you never heard of. Where you boys been?"

"At the jazz festival," I say proudly.

"No kidding. I used to play jazz."

"What instrument?" Russo asks.

"Piano."

"Where did you play?" I ask.

"All over."

"Why'd you stop playing?"

"Lost my timing."

1997

A light is on upstairs in my former writing teacher's house. The rest of the house is dark; the basement where she kept old clothes and the first floor where, sometimes, when I read my work aloud to her, I could anticipate her response.

I stand a moment longer and then walk to the corner bookstore and take Camus' first book, A Happy Death, *from the shelf. "For here is the young Camus himself, in love with the sea and sun, enraptured by women, yet disdainful of romantic love, and already formulating the philosophy of action and moral responsibility that would make him central to the thought of our time," the back cover reads.*

1957

A few days later, I take Nicole, the beatnik girl, to Hell, a coffee shop for beats. She's traveled with her father, a military man, and wears a beret and vest. We sit on huge pillows and listen to Charlie Parker on headphones. She leans her head on my shoulder. "Do you like jazz?"

I tell her about the jazz festival and the man.

"He was dying," she says.

"What do you mean?"

"He lost his timing."

Later, we walk to the lake. I take off my t-shirt and put it on the ground in the shadows of the pavilion. She gets down on her back and raises her arms to me. Her smile feathers my skin. I enter her and move back and forth the way Russo showed me. My body stretches and explodes. It's as if all of me flows into her.

> *He closed his eyes, surrendering himself to her, body and mind, conscious of nothing in the world but the dark pressure of her softly parting lips. They pressed upon his brain as upon his lips as though they were the vehicle of vague speech; and between them he felt the unknown and timid pressure, darker than the swoon of sin, softer than the sound of odour. (James Joyce,* A Portrait of the Artist as a Young Man*)*

1957

Afterward we look at the stars.

"Let's go for a swim," she says.

Clothes in hand we walk naked down the steps in front of the pavilion and climb over the rocks to the water. I hold her naked body a moment, then swim as far out as I can, head turned up at the night sky, then down into the dark water.

> *"He climbed up the ladder and wondered if he had the strength to get home. He had done what he wanted. He had swum the country, but was so stupefied with exhaustion that his triumph seemed vague." I read Cheever's "The Swimmer," see the movie starring Burt Lancaster, become fascinated with stories about men with something at the edge of their consciousness, something perhaps too painful or too beautiful to touch, like in a Sam Shepard play.*

BASKET HOLD (1972)

Daniel gets up from his chair and approaches, his t-shirt tattered and his face wind-burned from several days on the streets. He's 14.

"Mark." I hold out my hand.

He continues walking. I walk alongside and motion for him to enter an office.

"Hi Daniel, I'm Marjorie, your therapist." Marjorie, a new, young therapist, holds out her hand.

No response.

"Before Mark takes you upstairs I wanted to tell you a little about our program," Marjorie says.

"I don't give a fuck about the program!" He grabs a paperweight from Marjorie's desk, throws it through her window, and takes a swing at me. I duck and grab him around the waist and quick-step behind him, remembering my supervisor's instructions: "Grab both arms by the wrist and cross them in front of him, then put your knee behind his knee and dip like a basketball player taking the leap out of a rebounder in front of him, and collapse together to the floor. If he's small enough (Daniel is, just barely) sit him in front of you with your legs hooked over his so he can't kick, his body cradled in your arms, and your head tight to his so he can't butt you. Then prepare for a long wait. It helps to have something to support your back."

"Marjorie, would you move that couch over here?" My voice shakes. She gets on one end of the couch and pushes until it's between my back and the wall. He twists like a dog trying to avoid a bath and shouts: "Your mother sucks cock! Your ol' lady sleeps with horses, cows, pigs!" The veins in his neck cord and his body strains like a stretched bow. My arms begin to ache. The sweat thickens. His hand breaks free. He turns and spits, then butts me in the nose. "Damn!" Fireflies flash in my eyes. Blood begins to run down on my chin.

"Are you okay?" Marjorie asks.

"Yes, I think so. Would you please grab his legs?"

She straddles his legs and holds them to the ground while I retighten my grip, wishing I could pull his arms up around his neck and choke him. He rests, then jerks like a fish out of water, rests and jerks again until gradually he gives up and the tension subsides. We sit quietly, soaked in sweat, limbs intertwined, breaths as if coming from the same set of lungs and Marjorie connected to us by his legs.

"I'm going to let go of your left arm—then your right one." Step by step I release my hold until Daniel is standing across from me. Marjorie brings me a wet paper towel to wipe my nose and face. He shows no remorse.

"I'll take him upstairs," I say to Marjorie.

The living quarters are on the second floor. "Sticky suckers," Suzanne calls the smell of urine and disinfectant that I bring home each night. At the top of the stairs, I part the fire doors. The other boys are in school.

"Your room is down the hall," I say. He walks to my side and runs his shoulder along the wall. A grocery bag with his things is on the bed. He digs through it. "Bastards," he says. Ernie, my supervisor, searches all the new boys' things for drugs and weapons. Daniel takes out a t-shirt and pair of jeans, starts to change, then looks at me, "Mind."

I give him a moment to change and unpack, wait outside the door with my back to the wall, and question why I'm here.

1947

My mother stands on one side and my father on the other. We're on the ferryboat back to the mainland from the Statue of Liberty. In my hand is a small replica of the statue that I pleaded and begged for until my mother gave in. She's holding her large black straw hat to her head; her black and white polka dot dress and his gabardine pants blowing in the wind. I begin to think about how bad I would feel if the statue fell into the water.

"I don't know what gets into him," my mother says upon seeing the statue splash.

"Boys are like that," says my father as he stares out to sea.

1972

When I enter again he's sitting at the desk with a photo.

"Who's that?"

"None of your fuckin' business."

I don't respond.

"My sister."

"She's nice looking. What's this one?" It's a photo of Daniel in dancing tights.

"None of your business." He puts the photos in the drawer. "Why do you work here?"

"I'm not sure."

"So you can get your jollies, probably."

"Want a Coke?"

He nods and we walk to the day room.

I keep an eye on him as I buy Cokes from the vending machine, and then we sit across from one another at a small table. He sips his Coke, looks down, then up. "Your shoe's untied." He stares at me.

I stare back.

THE VISIT (1997)

A pick-up truck with a man sitting inside is parked in the driveway.

"Hello." His voice is deep and his complexion tanned or perhaps wind-burned.

"Daniel?"

"Yes." It's been more than 20 years since he ran away from the treatment center.

"Come inside." I give him a cold drink. He walks around the house with it in his hands looking at the paintings. "Where is she?"

"In New Mexico, painting."

"Your son?"

"Grown."

We sit down in the kitchen. "What brings you back?"

"Not sure."

"Have you been dancing?"

"No."

He walks into the living room and stares through the enclosed porch to the street.

"I was going for a run; want to come along?" I ask.

"Yes."

The air is clear, crisp. We run north along the shore, a route we took many times when he was at the group home. As we move together over the sidewalks, it is as if time stood still.

He rents an apartment, gets a road construction job, and tries, at age 37, to revive a dance career. We run together 2 or 3 times a week. One night, I stop by the dance studio. He walks over with a towel on his shoulders. The scars on his body seemed more pronounced.

"How long you been here?" he asks.

"Just a few minutes." We have coffee in a small shop next to the studio. It's raining a cold November rain.

"I saw my parents."

"How are they?"

"The same."

1973

Daniel gets up, pulls on his shorts, and leaves the tent. I follow, staying out of his sight. It's a warm August evening. We're (six boys from the treatment center and myself) camping in the Door Peninsula in Wisconsin.

When Daniel reaches the bluffs above Lake Michigan, he stands a moment and looks across the water. The moon is out. I duck behind a tall clump of grass. Suddenly he races down the dune and glides in long strides along the shore, puffs of sand forming behind him on the misty seaside stage. Then he charges up another dune using his arms as pistons and races down again. He repeats these glides and charges perhaps a dozen times until, exhausted, he collapses at the water's edge.

Caught up in the mood, I race down the dune hollering at the top of my lungs. Daniel stands and faces me. At the last moment I veer off and dive face first into the water. Daniel follows. We splash each other, swim in short bursts, then sit down with our chins on our knees.

"Do you think I'll be fucked up like my ol' man?" Daniel asks.

I hesitate. "No."

1997

Later, when I drop him off in front of his apartment above the hardware store, he says, "I'm not sure how long I'll stay. Will you come to see me perform?"

"Yes."

"Rhythmic interaction," I say.

The students look puzzled. We're sitting at a large round table on the second story of an old mansion that was given to the University.

"You mean in moments of connection?" a young man asks.

"Yes," I reply.

"You mean like dancing?"

"Yes."

We're discussing how to form connections with troubled youth and a scene from my novel about Daniel, who became a modern dancer. The book was published two years earlier. It is not required reading, but some of the students found it in the bookstore and the word got out.

"So is this novel about you or Daniel?" a student asks.

"It's fiction."

"Yes, we know, but there are parts of people you knew in the characters."

I smile.

1997

Earlier in the year, I put Camus back on the shelf and walk toward the lake. A foghorn sounds in the distance. For a moment I think I see her: the writing teacher–handsome woman with the premature gray hair and baby skin–but it's someone else.

1997

The performance is held in an eastside loft. Several students from the class I teach on adolescent development sit with me on folding chairs as Daniel takes the stage and moves to composer John Adams' aching harmonies. It is an acrobatic, if not graceful, performance. His steps are bold, strong with pain, anger, and relief, but not as intense or free as when he was younger.

"I wish I could dance like that," a student says as we stand together outside. Her face is naked, innocent.

"He's gone," the landlord says a few days later.

"Did he say where?"

"No, he just paid his rent and left."

> *I do not know what the spirit of a philosopher could more wish to be than a good dancer. For the dance is his ideal, also his art, finally also the only kind of piety he knows, his divine spirit. (Nietzsche)*

2000

I run home along Lake Michigan past the place I was before. The sunbather is out, shielded from the wind by reflectors. I wave. He waves back. For a moment he and I brave winter alone. I continue, lost in the rhythm of my gait. Rafts of ice push up along the shore. Near the water purification plant I enter a ravine that rises to the pavilion. Away from the wind and traffic I can hear my feet hit the ground like a distant heart-beat. I rest a moment where the sun filters through the barren elms and then climb the steps to the pavilion and look down into the cold water I once swam in on warm summer nights.

Pavilion: A temporary shelter; the external ear–place as in the place that is one's self.

EPILOGUE

Youthwork is like a modern dance. We bring ourselves to the moment and try to interact in synch with youth's rhythms for trusting and growing. As we interact we are in a sense in and passing through youth. The challenge is to know ourselves so that we can know others, and this comes about in part through a constant exploration of our stories. It also comes about when we are in youthwork with youth, learning how to dance.

References and Recommended Readings

Baizerman, M. (1998). From here to there, from then to now, along these roads and paths. *Child and Youth Care Forum, 27,* 441-446. (Also see his column, Musing with Mike in the *Child and Youth Care Forum,* 1990-2000)

Baizerman, M. (1995). Kids, place, and action(less). *Child and Youth Care Forum, 24,* 339-341.

Baizerman, M. (1992). Book review of *Buckets: sketches from the log book of a youth worker* by Mark Krueger. *Child and Youth Care Forum, 21,* 129-133.

Beker, J. (1998). The best is yet to come. *Child and Youth Care Forum, 27,* 381-382.

Beker, J. (1996). Introduction: calling our bluff. *Child and Youth Care Forum, 25,* 277-279.

Beker, J., & Eisikovits, Z. (Eds.) (1992). *Knowledge utilization in residential child and youth care.* Washington, DC: Child Welfare League of America.

Bruner, J. (1996). *The culture of education.* Cambridge, MA: Harvard University Press.

Bruner, J. (1990). *Acts of meaning.* Cambridge, MA: Harvard University Press.

Carver, R. (1983). *Fires.* New York: Vintage Press.

Childress, H. (2000). *Landscapes of betrayal, landscapes of joy: Curtisville in the lives of its teenagers.* New York: Albany. State University of New York Press.

Craig, E. (1978). The heart of the teacher: a heuristic study of the inner world of teaching. *Dissertation Abstracts International, 38,* 7222A.

Crain, W. (1999). *Theories of human development: concepts and applications.* Edgewood Cliffs, NJ: Prentice Hall.

Dejardins, S., & Freeman, A. (1991). Out of synch. *Journal of Child and Youth Care, 6,* 139-144.

Ducornet, R. (2002). The deep zoo. *Conjunctions, 38,* 14-23.

Edelshick, T. (1998). Entering play: lesson in grief, joy, and life. In M. Nukalla & S. Ravitch (Eds.), *Matters of interpretation* (pp. 276-291). San Francisco: Jossey Bass Publishers.

Fahlberg, V. (1990). *Residential treatment: a tapestry of many therapies.* Indianapolis: Perspectives Press.

Fay, M. (1989). *Speak out.* Toronto: Pape Adolescent Center.

Fewster, G. (1999). Turning myself inside out: my theory of me. *Journal of Child and Youth Care, 13,* 35-54.

Fewster, G. (1990). *Being in child care: a journey into self.* New York: The Haworth Press, Inc.

Fulcher, L. (1999). The soul, rhythm, and blues of residential child care practice. *Journal of Child and Youth Care, 4,* 13-28.

Garfat, T. (2001). Editorial: congruence between supervision and practice. *Journal of Child and Youth Care, 15,* iii-v.

http://www.haworthpress.com/web/CYS
© 2004 by The Haworth Press, Inc. All rights reserved.
Digital Object Identifier: 10.1300/J024v26n01_06

Garfat, T. (1998). The effective child and youth care intervention. *Journal of Child and Youth Care, 12*, 1-178.

Garfat, T. (1991). Footprints on the boarder of reality. *Journal of Child and Youth Care, 6*, 157-160.

Goffman, E. (1959). *The presentation of self in everyday life.* New York: Doubleday.

Guttman, E. (1991). Immediacy in residential child and youth care: the fusion of experience, self-consciousness, and action. In J. Beker and Z. Eisikovits (Eds.), *Knowledge utilization in residential child and youth care practice.* Washington, DC: Child Welfare League of America.

Hall, E. (1976). *Beyond culture.* Garden City, NY: Anchor Books.

Husserl, E. (1970). *Logical investigations.* New York: Humanities Press.

Krueger, M. (1998). *Interactive youth work practice.* Washington, DC: Child Welfare League of America.

Krueger, M. (1997). Using self, story, and intuition to understand child and youth care work. *Child and Youth Care Forum, 26*, 153-161.

Krueger, M. (1995). *Nexus: a book about youth work.* Washington, DC: Child Welfare League of America.

Krueger, M. (1987). *Floating.* Washington, DC: Child Welfare League of America.

Krueger, M., & Stuart, C. (1999). Context and competence in work with children and youth. *Child and Youth Care Forum, 28*(3), 195-204.

Magnuson, D., Baizerman, M., & Stringer, A. (2001). A moral praxis of child and youth care work. *Journal of Child and Youth Care Work, 15-16*, 302-313.

Maier, H. (1995). Genuine child and youth care practice across the North American continent. *Journal of Child and Youth Care, 10*, 11-22.

Maier, H. (1992). Rhythmicity–A powerful force for experiencing unity and personal connections. *Journal of Child and Youth Care Work, 8*, 7-13.

Maier, H. (1987). *Development group care of children and youth: concepts and practice.* New York: The Haworth Press, Inc.

Moustakas, C. (1994). *Phenomenological research methods.* University of Chicago Press.

Moustakas, C. (1990). *Heuristic research.* Newberry Park, CA.: Sage Publications.

Nakkula, M., & Ravitch, S. (1998). *Matters of interpretation.* San Francisco: Jossey-Bass Publishers.

Nygen, P. (1992). Journal at the shelter. *Child and Youth Care Forum, 21*, 91-104.

Ortiz, S. (1992). *Woven stone.* Tucson: University of Arizona Press.

Peterson, R. (1994). The adrenaline metaphor: narrative mind and practice in child and child and youth care. *Journal of Child and Youth Care, 9*(2), 107-122.

Phelan, J. (2001). Experiential counseling and the CYC practitioner. *Journal of Child and Youth Care Work, 15-16*, 257-264.

Rapoport, A. (1990). *The meaning of the built environment.* Tucson: University of Arizona Press.

Redl, F., & Wineman, D. (1952). *Controls from within: techniques for the treatment of the aggressive child.* New York: Free Press.

Richardson, L. (2000). Writing: a method of inquiry. In K. Denzin, & Y. Lincoln (Eds.), *Handbook of qualitative research* (pp. 923-948). Thousand Oaks, CA.

Rose Sladde, L. (1996). Journal entries. *Journal of Child and Youth Care, 10*(4), 79-83.

Saleebey, D. (1994). Culture, theory, and narrative: the intersection of meanings in practice. *Social Work, 39*(4), 35-359.

Sarris, G. (1993). *Keeping slug woman alive: an holistic approach to American Indian texts.* Berkeley: University of California Press.

Vander Ven, K. (1999a). Postmodern thought and its relevance to child and youth care work. *Child and Youth Care Forum, 28,* 294-301.

Vander Ven, K. (1999b). You are what you do and become what you've done: the role of activity in the development of self. *Journal of Child and Youth Care, 13,* 133-147.

Vander Ven, K. (1995). Point and level systems: another way to fail children and youth. *Child and Youth Care Forum, 24,* 347-365.

Van Manen, M. (1990). *Researching lived experience: human science for an action sensitive pedagogy.* Albany, NY: State University of New York.

Vygotsky, L.S. (1978). *Mind in society.* Cambridge, MA: Harvard University Press.

Ward-Harrison, S. (1999). *Spilling open: the art of becoming yourself.* Novoto, CA: New World Library.

Index

Social Skills Training for Children and Youth, edited by Craig LeCroy, MSW (Vol. 5, No. 3/4, 1983). *"Easy to read and pertinent to occupational therapists." (New Zealand Journal of Occupational Therapy)*

Legal Reforms Affecting Child and Youth Services, edited by Gary B. Melton, PhD (Vol. 5, No. 1/2, 1983). *"A consistently impressive book. The authors bring a wealth of empirical data and creative legal analyses to bear on one of the most important topics in psychology and law." (John Monahan, School of Law, University of Virginia)*

Youth Participation and Experiential Education, edited by Daniel Conrad and Diane Hedin (Vol. 4, No. 3/4, 1982). *A useful introduction and overview of the current and possible future impact of experiential education on adolescents.*

Institutional Abuse of Children and Youth, edited by Ranae Hanson (Vol. 4, No. 1/2, 1982). *"Well researched . . . should be required reading for every school administrator, school board member, teacher, and parent." (American Psychological Association Division 37 Newsletter)*

BOOK ORDER FORM!

Order a copy of this book with this form or online at:
http://www.haworthpress.com/store/product.asp?sku=5316

Themes and Stories in Youthwork Practice

____ in softbound at $17.95 (ISBN: 0-7890-2582-5)
____ in hardbound at $34.95 (ISBN: 0-7890-2581-7)

COST OF BOOKS ____	❏**BILL ME LATER:**
	Bill-me option is good on US/Canada/ Mexico orders only; not good to jobbers,
POSTAGE & HANDLING ____	wholesalers, or subscription agencies.
US: $4.00 for first book & $1.50 for each additional book. Outside US: $5.00 for first book & $2.00 for each additional book.	❏**Signature** ____
	❏ **Payment Enclosed: $** ____
SUBTOTAL ____	❏ **PLEASE CHARGE TO MY CREDIT CARD:**
In Canada: add 7% GST. ____	❏Visa ❏MasterCard ❏AmEx ❏Discover
STATE TAX ____	❏Diner's Club ❏Eurocard ❏JCB
CA, IL, IN, MN, NJ, NY, OH & SD residents please add appropriate local sales tax.	**Account #** ____
FINAL TOTAL ____	**Exp Date** ____
If paying in Canadian funds, convert using the current exchange rate, UNESCO coupons welcome.	**Signature** ____
	(Prices in US dollars and subject to change without notice.)

PLEASE PRINT ALL INFORMATION OR ATTACH YOUR BUSINESS CARD

Name
Address
City   State/Province   Zip/Postal Code
Country
Tel   Fax
E-Mail

May we use your e-mail address for confirmations and other types of information? ❏Yes ❏No We appreciate receiving your e-mail address. Haworth would like to e-mail special discount offers to you, as a preferred customer. **We will never share, rent, or exchange your e-mail address.** We regard such actions as an invasion of your privacy.

Order From Your **Local Bookstore** or Directly From
The Haworth Press, Inc. 10 Alice Street, Binghamton, New York 13904-1580 • USA
Call Our toll-free number (1-800-429-6784) / Outside US/Canada: (607) 722-5857
Fax: 1-800-895-0582 / Outside US/Canada: (607) 771-0012
E-mail your order to us: orders@haworthpress.com

For orders outside US and Canada, you may wish to order through your local
sales representative, distributor, or bookseller.
For information, see http://haworthpress.com/distributors

(Discounts are available for individual orders in US and Canada only, not booksellers/distributors.)

Please photocopy this form for your personal use.
www.HaworthPress.com

BOF04